P · O · C · K · E · T · S

SPACE FACTS

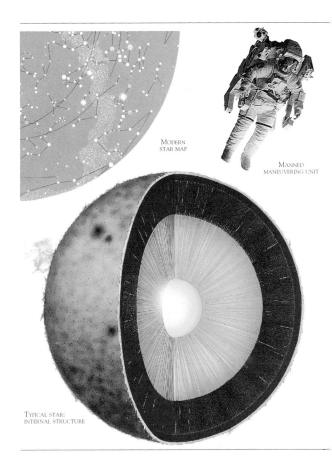

MODERN
STAR MAP

MANNED
MANEUVERING UNIT

TYPICAL STAR:
INTERNAL STRUCTURE

P · O · C · K · E · T · S

SPACE FACTS

Written by
CAROLE STOTT and
CLINT TWIST

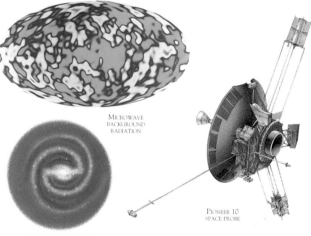

MICROWAVE
BACKGROUND
RADIATION

PIONEER 10
SPACE PROBE

BARRED SPIRAL GALAXY

A DK PUBLISHING BOOK

Project editor	Clint Twist
Art editor	Alexandra Brown
Senior editor	Laura Buller
Senior art editor	Helen Senior
Editorial consultant	Carole Stott
Picture research	Fiona Watson
Production	Louise Barratt
US editor	Jill Hamilton
US consultant	Dr. William A. Gutsch
	Hayden Planetarium,
	American Museum of Natural History

This book is dedicated to the memory of Janet MacLennan

First American Edition, 1995
6 8 10 9 7
Published in the United States by
DK Publishing, Inc.,
95 Madison Avenue, New York, New York 10016

Visit us on the World Wide Web at http://www.dk.com

Copyright © 1995 Dorling Kindersley Ltd., London

Library of Congress Cataloging-in-Publication Data

Stott, Carole.
    Space facts / by Carole Stott and Clint Twist – 1st Amer. ed.
        p. cm. — (A DK pocket)
    Includes index.
    ISBN 1–56458–892–0
  1. Space sciences–Handbooks, manuals, etc.– Juvenile literature.
  2. Astronomy–Handbooks, manuals, etc.–Juvenile literature.
  [1. Space sciences. 2. Astronomy.] I.Title. II. Series.
QB500.22.S76 1995
500.5–dc20
                                           94-24740
                                           CIP
                                           AC

Color reproduction by Colourscan, Singapore
Printed and bound in Italy by L.E.G.O.

CONTENTS

HOW TO USE THIS BOOK

These pages show you how to use *Pockets: Space Facts*.
The book is divided into nine sections. Each section
contains information on one aspect of space or space
exploration. At the beginning of each section there
is a picture page and a guide to the contents of
that section.

OBJECTS IN SPACE

Some of the sections deal with
objects in space, such as galaxies,
stars, and planets. Other sections
deal with the appearance of these
objects in Earth's sky.

CORNER CODING
The page corners
are color coded
according to
the section.

	UNIVERSE
	GALAXIES
	STARS
	SPACE FROM EARTH
	SOLAR SYSTEM
	PLANETS
	SMALL OBJECTS
	STUDYING SPACE
	SPACE HISTORY

Corner coding

Heading →

Introduction →

PLANETS

SATURN
FAMED FOR ITS magnificent
ring system, Saturn is the
second largest of the planets.
Like its nearest neighbor
Jupiter, Saturn is a gas
giant. However, the mass
is so spread out that on
average the planet is less
dense than water. Saturn has
more moons than any other
planet – at least 18. The
largest moon, Titan, has an
unusually thick atmosphere.

RINGED WORLD
Saturn is at the limit of easy
telescope viewing from
Earth. This photograph was
taken at a distance of
11 million miles (17.5 million
km) by Voyager 2.

Earth   Saturn

SATURN: PLANETARY DATA	
Average distance from the Sun	886.9 million miles
	1,427 million km
Orbital period	29.46 Earth years
Orbital velocity	6 miles/sec (9.6 km/s)
Rotation period	10.23 hours
Diameter at equator	74,914 miles (120,536 km)
Mass (Earth = 1)	95
Gravity (Earth = 1)	0.93
Number of moons	18

SATURN FACTS
• Saturn's rings are less
than 656 ft (200 m)
thick, but over 167,80
miles (270,000 km) in
diameter.
• The rings consist
of billions of ice-
covered rock
fragments and
dust particles.

Data box →

Fact box →

HEADING
This describes the
subject of the page.
This page is about
Saturn. If a subject
continues over
several pages, the
same heading applies.

DATA BOXES
Some pages have data
boxes. These contain
detailed numerical
information, such as
the distances between
galaxies, stars, planets,
and moons. This data is
often set out in tables.

FACT BOXES
Many pages have fact boxes.
These contain at-a-glance
information about the subjec
such as the temperature at th
core of a typical star, or the
brightest planet in Earth's sk

Introduction

This provides you with a summary and overview of the subject. After reading the introduction, you should have a clear idea of what the following page, or pages, are about.

Running heads

These remind you which section you are in. The top of the left-hand page gives the section name. The right-hand page gives the subject. This page on Saturn is from the planets section.

Captions and annotations

Most illustrations have an explanatory caption. Annotations, in *italics*, draw your attention to particular features of an illustration and usually have leader lines.

Caption

Running head

Label

Annotation

Numbers

Large numbers are often given in standard scientific notation – as a number with just one digit left of the decimal point multiplied by a power of ten. For example, $1.8 \times 10^9 = 1.8 \times 10 \times 10 \times 10 \times 10 \times 10 \times 10 \times 10 \times 10$.

Greek alphabet

Greek letters are used to identify stars.

α	alpha	ν	nu
β	beta	ξ	xi
γ	gamma	o	omicron
δ	delta	π	pi
ε	epsilon	ρ	rho
ζ	zeta	σ	sigma
η	eta	τ	tau
θ	theta	υ	upsilon
ι	iota	φ	phi
κ	kappa	χ	chi
λ	lambda	ψ	psi

Labels

For extra clarity, some pictures have labels. The labels may identify a picture when it is not obvious from the text what it is, or may give extra information about the subject.

Index and glossary

There is a subject index at the back of the book which alphabetically lists every subject. There is also an alphabetical glossary that explains the meaning of the scientific and technical terms used in this book.

UNIVERSE

WHAT IS THE UNIVERSE?

THE UNIVERSE IS EVERYTHING that exists. From the Earth beneath our feet to the farthest stars, everything is a part of the universe. The universe is so large that it contains countless billions of stars. However, most of it consists of nothing but empty space.

Galaxies

Galaxy containing billions of stars

Supernova – the death of a large star

Comet – a dirty snowball

LOOKING TO THE SKIES

From Earth, we can look into space and study the universe. In every direction we look there are stars. There are more stars in the universe than any other type of object – stars at different stages of their lives in enormous groups called galaxies, including at least one star that has planets. Despite the huge size of the universe, we know of only one place where life exists – planet Earth.

UNIVERSE FACTS

• There are about 100 billion galaxies in the universe; each contains approximately 1 billion stars.

• The most distant objects we can detect are 87,000 million million million miles (139,000 million million million km) away.

HORSEHEAD IN SPACE
Looking like a chess knight, the Horsehead
Nebula (center left) is a gigantic cloud of dark-
colored dust. It is visible because the dust blocks
out light from behind the nebula, so that we see it
in silhouette. The universe contains many similar
clouds that block our view of different regions.

Pulsar – a rapidly
rotating neutron star

The Sun –
an ordinary
middle-aged star

Cluster
of stars

Quasar –
a very bright and
distant object

Planets – balls of
rock, ice, or gas

Nebula – a cloud
of gas and dust

VISUALIZING THE UNIVERSE
The easiest way to think of the universe
is as a sphere which is constantly
expanding so that everything is getting
farther away from everything else. There
is nothing beyond the universe, because
the universe contains all of time and
space within it.

SCALE OF THE UNIVERSE

DISTANCES IN THE UNIVERSE are so great that the light-year is used as a unit of measurement. Light travels at about 186,000 miles/sec (300,000 km/s), and a light-year (ly) is the distance light travels in one year. A galaxy can measure thousands of light-years across and be millions of light-years distant.

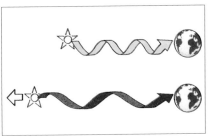

LIGHT AND MOTION
A star's light can tell us about its motion. If the star is moving away from Earth, its light is stretched by comparison with stationary stars. Light from a star moving away is also shifted toward the red end of the spectrum. Stars approaching Earth have compressed light shifted toward blue.

SCALE OF SIZES
The human world, the world of everyday experience, is dwarfed by the scale of the universe. Earth is one of nine planets orbiting the Sun, which is one of about 200 billion stars in the Milky Way galaxy.

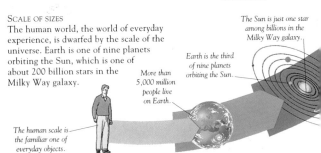

The Sun is just one star among billions in the Milky Way galaxy.

Earth is the third of nine planets orbiting the Sun.

More than 5,000 million people live on Earth.

The human scale is the familiar one of everyday objects.

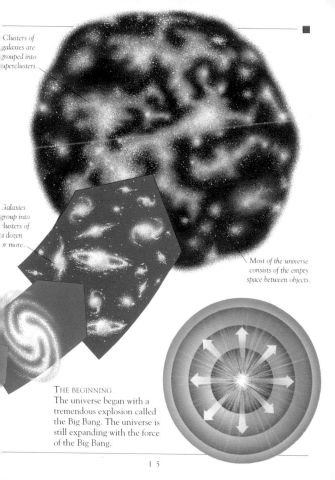

Clusters of
galaxies are
grouped into
superclusters.

Galaxies
group into
clusters of
a dozen
or more.

Most of the universe
consists of the empty
space between objects.

THE BEGINNING
The universe began with a
tremendous explosion called
the Big Bang. The universe is
still expanding with the force
of the Big Bang.

LIFE STORY OF THE UNIVERSE

ALL MATTER, ENERGY, space, and time were created in
the Big Bang around 15 billion years ago. At first the
universe was small and very hot. Atomic particles
joined to form hydrogen and helium and the universe
expanded and cooled. Over millions of years these
gases have produced galaxies, stars, planets, and us.

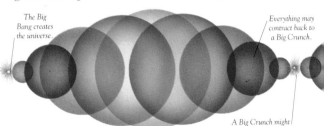

The Big Bang creates the universe.

Everything may contract back to a Big Crunch.

A Big Crunch might be followed by another Big Bang.

WHAT HAPPENS NEXT?
There are two theories about the future of
the universe. Either it will stop expanding
and shrink back in a process called a Big
Crunch, or carry on expanding forever.

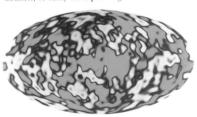

BIG BANG RIPPLES
This map of the whole sky is
based on tiny variations in
the temperature of space.
Red is warmer than average
and blue is colder. These
tiny variations are
irregularities of the Big Bang
explosion. The information
for the map was obtained by
the Cosmic Background
Explorer Satellite (COBE).

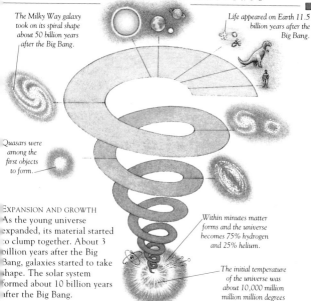

The Milky Way galaxy took on its spiral shape about 50 billion years after the Big Bang.

Life appeared on Earth 11.5 billion years after the Big Bang.

Quasars were among the first objects to form.

EXPANSION AND GROWTH
As the young universe expanded, its material started to clump together. About 3 billion years after the Big Bang, galaxies started to take shape. The solar system formed about 10 billion years after the Big Bang.

Within minutes matter forms and the universe becomes 75% hydrogen and 25% helium.

The initial temperature of the universe was about 10,000 million million million degrees

UNIVERSE: COOLING DATA	
Time after Big Bang	Temperature
10^{-6} secs	1.8×10^{13}°F (10^{13}°C)
3 minutes	1.8×10^{8}°F (10^{8}°C)
300,000 years	10,000°C-18,000°F (10^{4}°C)
1 million years	5,400°F (3,000°C)
1,000 million years	−275°F (−170°C)
15,000 million years	−454°F (−270°C)

UNIVERSE FACT
• Scientists can trace the life story of the universe back to what is called the Planck time, 10^{-43} seconds after the Big Bang.
10^{-43} means a decimal point followed by 42 zeros and then a one.

GALAXIES

WHAT IS A GALAXY?

A GALAXY IS an enormous group of stars. A large galaxy may have a billion, a small galaxy only a few hundred thousand. Even small galaxies are so big that it takes light thousands of years to cross them. Galaxies are formed from vast spinning clouds of gas. Many continue to spin. The speed of rotation affects their shape.

DISTANT STAR CITY
The Andromeda galaxy is so far away that its light takes 2,200,000 years to travel to Earth. We see the galaxy as it was 2,200,000 years ago.

GALAXIES: THE FOUR BASIC TYPES

ELLIPTICAL
These range from ball-shaped to egg-shaped. They contain mainly old stars, and are the most common type.

SPIRAL
These are disk-shaped. Most material is in the spiral arms where new stars are formed. Old stars are in the nucleus.

BARRED-SPIRAL
These are like spiral galaxies, but the nucleus is elongated into a bar. The spiral arms extend from the ends of the bar.

BRIGHTEST LIGHTS
This is an X-ray image of a quasi-stellar object, one of the brightest, and remotest objects. The most distant are about 15 billion light-years away. Known as quasars, they are probably the cores of the first galaxies to be formed.

BRIGHT GALAXIES: DATA		
Galaxy	Distance	Type
Andromeda (M31)	2,200,000 ly	Sb
M32	2,300,000 ly	E2
M33	2,400,000 ly	Sc
Wolf-Lundmark	4,290,000 ly	Irr
M81	9,450,000 ly	Sb
Centaurus A	13,040,000 ly	E0
Pinwheel (M101)	23,790,000 ly	Sc
Whirlpool (M51)	29,340,000 ly	Sc
NGC2841	37,490,000 ly	Sb
NGC1023	39,120,000 ly	E7
NGC3184	42,380,000 lv	Sc
NGC5866	42,380,000 ly	E6
M100	48,900,000 ly	Sc
NGC6643	74,980,000 ly	Sc
M77	81,500,000 ly	Sb
NGC3938	94,540,000 ly	Sc
NGC2207	114,100,000 ly	Sc

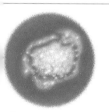

IRREGULAR
Some of these have a hint of spiral structure, while others do not fit any known pattern. They are the rarest type.

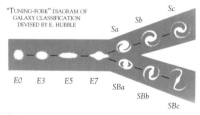

"TUNING-FORK" DIAGRAM OF
GALAXY CLASSIFICATION
DEVISED BY E. HUBBLE

Sc
Sb
Sa
E0 E3 E5 E7
SBa
SBb
SBc

CLASSIFYING GALAXIES BY SHAPE
Elliptical galaxies are classified from E0 (spherical) to E7 (very flattened). Spirals (S) and barred spirals (SB) are graded from a to c, according to the compactness of the central nucleus and the tightness of the arms. Irregular galaxies (Irr) are not shown here, but can be divided into types I and II.

CLUSTERS AND SUPERCLUSTERS

GALAXIES OCCUR TOGETHER in clusters that range in size from a few to a few thousand galaxies. Clusters themselves also occur in groups called superclusters, which are the largest structures in the universe.

NEIGHBORING CLUSTER
The Virgo cluster is about 60 million light-years away, but it is the nearest major cluster to our own Local Group.

Milky Way

M31

M33

THE LOCAL GROUP
Our own cluster is about five million light-years across and contains about 30 galaxies. The largest galaxies in the Local Group are Andromeda (M31), Triangulum (M33), and our own Milky Way galaxy.

SUPERCLUSTER FACTS

• The average distance between galaxies in a cluster is about ten galaxy diameters.

• The Local Group is just one small part of a giant supercluster about 100 million light-years in diameter.

SOME LOCAL GROUP GALAXIES: DATA

Name	Diameter	Distance
Andromeda	150,000 ly	2,200,000 ly
M33	40,000 ly	2,400,000 ly
Large Magellanic Cloud (LMC)	30,000 ly	170,000 ly
Small Magellanic Cloud (SMC)	20,000 ly	190,000 ly
NGC 6822	15,000 ly	1,800,000 ly
NGC 205	11,000 ly	2,200,000 ly

HONEYCOMB SPACE

Superclusters tend to be flattened into disks or sheets, or elongated into filaments. These shapes cannot be seen through a telescope, but scientists now know that the large-scale structure of the universe is basically a honeycomb arrangement. Superclusters are arranged on the surface of immense "bubbles." These bubbles are almost completely empty of matter. They are huge voids that contain only a few atoms of gas.

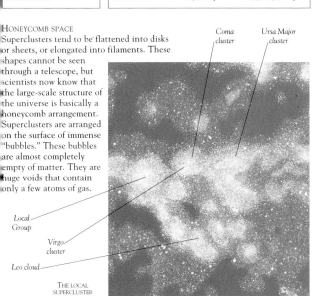

Coma cluster

Ursa Major cluster

Local Group

Virgo cluster

Leo cloud

THE LOCAL SUPERCLUSTER

THE MILKY WAY

THE SUN IS JUST ONE of about 200 billion stars in our own galaxy – the Milky Way. Ours is a spiral galaxy, with a nucleus of old stars surrounded by a halo of even older stars. All the young stars, such as the Sun, are located in the spiral arms. The Milky Way is so large that it takes light 100,000 years to travel from edge to edge. All the stars we see at night are in the Milky Way.

SAGITTARIUS STAR CLOUD
This photograph shows young stars in a small part of the Sagittarius arm of the Milky Way. Clouds of dust obscure our view of most of that region of the galaxy.

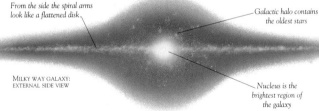

From the side the spiral arms look like a flattened disk

Galactic halo contains the oldest stars

MILKY WAY GALAXY:
EXTERNAL SIDE VIEW

Nucleus is the brightest region of the galaxy

SIDE-ON SPIRAL
Viewed from the side, from a distance of about a million light-years, the Milky Way galaxy would look like a giant lens – with flattened edges and a bright central nucleus. Around the nucleus is a roughly spherical halo that contains the oldest stars in the galaxy.

THE MILKY WAY
AS SEEN FROM
EARTH

ABOVE THE SPIRAL
From above, or below, the spiral arms of
the Milky Way galaxy would be clearly
visible. These contain most of the galaxy's
gas and dust, and this is where
star-forming regions
are found.

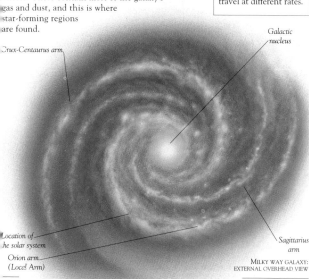

Crux-Centaurus arm

Galactic
nucleus

Location of
the solar system

Orion arm
(Local Arm)

Sagittarius
arm

MILKY WAY GALAXY:
EXTERNAL OVERHEAD VIEW

2 5

THE LOCAL ARM

THE SOLAR SYSTEM is situated about two-thirds of the
way from the galaxy's center, at the edge of a spiral
arm called the Local Arm or the Orion Arm. From
this viewpoint, we see the galaxy as a great milky
river of stars across
the night sky.

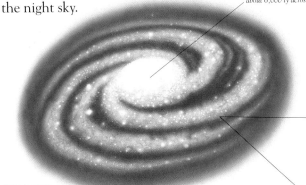

*The galactic nucleus is
about 6,000 ly across.*

POSITION OF THE
LOCAL ARM IN
THE GALAXY

SEVEN STARRY SISTERS
The Pleiades is a cluster of bright stars,
seven of which can be seen with the naked
eye, hence their popular name – the Seven
Sisters – which has been in use for at least
2,000 years. In fact there are more than 200
stars in the cluster, which formed about 60
million years ago – shortly after the
dinosaurs died out on Earth.

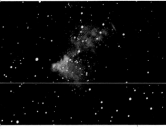

SPECTACULAR END

The Dumbbell Nebula, located about 1,000 light-years from the Sun, is a single star nearing the end of its life. Spherical shells of gas are blown out from the star's surface, making a spectacular sight. Gradually the gas will disperse, and will eventually be used to form new stars elsewhere in the galaxy.

LOCAL ARM FACTS

• From edge to edge the Dumbbell Nebula is two light-years in diameter.

• Some stars in Canis Major are only about 300,000 years old – mere star babies compared with our 5 billion-year-old Sun.

• The nearest bright star cluster to the Sun is the Hyades about 150 light-years away. The Hyades forms the V-shape of the bull's head in the constellation of Taurus.

THE LOCAL REGION OF SPACE WITHIN 1,000 LIGHT-YEARS OF THE SUN

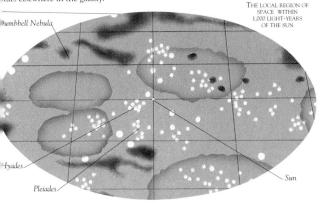

Dumbbell Nebula

Hyades

Pleiades

Sun

STARS

WHAT IS A STAR?

A STAR IS an enormous spinning ball of hot and luminous gas. Most stars contain two main gases – hydrogen and helium. These gases are held together by gravity, and at the core they are very densely packed. Within the core, immense amounts of energy are produced.

STAR CLUSTER
The cluster M13 in the constellation of Hercules contains hundreds of thousands of stars arranged in a compact ball.

STRUCTURE OF A STAR

Temperature and pressure increase toward the core.

Energy is released at the surface as light and heat.

Energy is produced by nuclear reactions in the core

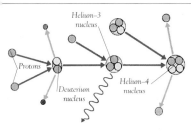

CORE FUSION
A star produces energy by nuclear fusion. Within the core, hydrogen nuclei (protons) collide and fuse to form first deuterium (heavy hydrogen) and then two forms of helium. During fusion, energy is given off. This type of reaction, which is found in most stars, is called the proton-proton chain.

VARYING SIZES
Stars differ greatly in the amount of gas they contain, and in their size. The largest stars are 1,000 times the diameter of the Sun, while the smallest are just a fraction of its size – not much bigger than the planet Jupiter.

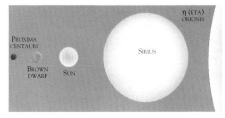

PROMINENT STARS: DATA		
Name	Designation	Distance
Vega	α Lyrae	26 ly
Pollux	β Geminorum	36 ly
Capella	α Aurigae	45 ly
Aldebaran	α Tauri	68 ly
Regulus	α Leonis	84 ly
Canopus	α Carinae	98 ly
Spica	α Virginis	260 ly
Betelgeuse	α Orionis	520 ly
Polaris	α Ursa Minoris	700 ly

STAR FACTS
• All the chemical elements heavier than hydrogen, helium, and lithium were made by nuclear reactions inside stars.
• The mass of the Sun – 1 solar mass – is used as a standard for measuring other stars.

STAR BIRTH

STARS FOLLOW a life cycle that lasts millions to billions of years. All stars begin in the same way – as material in a nebula, a cloud of gas and dust. Stars are not born individually, but in groups called clusters. Initially, the stars in a cluster have roughly the same composition. Despite these early similarities, the stars usually develop at different rates, and most clusters drift apart before very long.

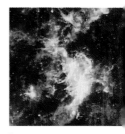

STELLAR BIRTHPLACE
In the Orion Nebula light from new stars illuminates the dust clouds. The stars themselves remain hidden by the dust. One of these young stars is 10,000 times brighter than the Sun.

FORMATION AND EARLY DEVELOPMENT OF A STAR

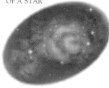

Inside a nebula, gravity causes spinning balls of gas to form – these are known as protostars.

The protostar (seen here in cross-section) shrinks, and its core becomes denser. An outer halo of gas and dust develops.

When the core reaches critical density, nuclear reactions start. The energy released blows away most of the halo.

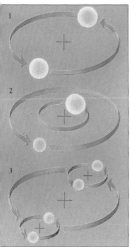

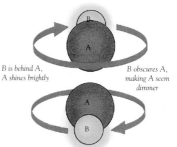

SINGLE OR DOUBLE

The Sun is unusual – it is a solitary star. In most cases a protostar spins fast enough to form a double or multiple star (1). Multiple stars may orbit around a common center of gravity (2), and may also orbit around one another (3). Double stars often appear to be variable in their light output because one star regularly blocks the light of the other.

B is behind A,
A shines brightly

B obscures A,
making A seem
dimmer

As the young star continues to spin rapidly, the remaining gas and dust become flattened into a disk.

In at least one case (the star we call the Sun) this disk of gas and dust has formed into a system of orbiting planets.

With or without planets, the new star now shines steadily, converting hydrogen to helium by nuclear fusion.

LIFE CYCLE OF A STAR

A STAR'S LIFE CYCLE depends on its mass. Stars of the same mass as the Sun shine steadily for about 10 billion years. More massive stars convert their hydrogen more quickly, and have shorter lives. The Sun is halfway through its life. In about 5 billion years, it will expand to become a red giant star, and then collapse and end as a dwarf star.

Star converting hydrogen i.e. in the main sequence

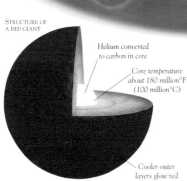

STRUCTURE OF A RED GIANT

Helium converted to carbon in core

Core temperature about 180 million°F (100 million°C)

Cooler outer layers glow red

RED GIANTS

When most of the hydrogen has been converted to helium, the star becomes a red giant – converting helium to carbon. The core heats up causing the surface to expand and cool. A red giant may expand to more than 100 times its former size.

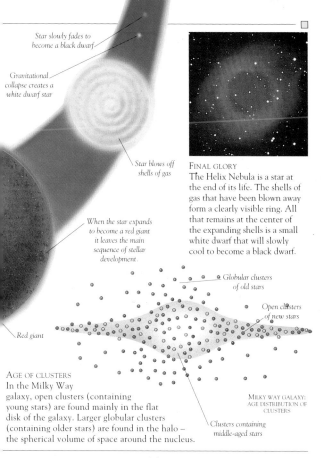

Star slowly fades to become a black dwarf

Gravitational collapse creates a white dwarf star

Star blows off shells of gas

When the star expands to become a red giant it leaves the main sequence of stellar development.

Red giant

FINAL GLORY

The Helix Nebula is a star at the end of its life. The shells of gas that have been blown away form a clearly visible ring. All that remains at the center of the expanding shells is a small white dwarf that will slowly cool to become a black dwarf.

Globular clusters of old stars

Open clusters of new stars

Clusters containing middle-aged stars

MILKY WAY GALAXY: AGE DISTRIBUTION OF CLUSTERS

AGE OF CLUSTERS

In the Milky Way galaxy, open clusters (containing young stars) are found mainly in the flat disk of the galaxy. Larger globular clusters (containing older stars) are found in the halo – the spherical volume of space around the nucleus.

DEATH OF MASSIVE STARS

THE WAY A STAR DIES depends on its mass. The most massive stars end their lives by simply exploding. This huge explosion is called a supernova, and may be bright enough to briefly outshine an entire galaxy. What happens next depends on how much stellar material is left after the supernova.

EXPLOSIVE COLLAPSE
Stars of at least eight solar masses end as supernovae. Gravity causes them to collapse with incredible force producing shock waves.

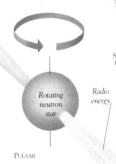

SUPERNOVA
EXPLOSION

Temperature at core 18 billion°F (10 billion°C)

Radio energy

Rotating neutron star

PULSAR

NEUTRON SPINNER
If the core that remains after a supernova is between 1.4 and 3.0 solar masses, it forms what is called a neutron star. Composed of super-dense material, neutron stars spin very quickly and produce beams of radio energy that appear to flash on and off very rapidly. These are called pulsars.

A RARE AND SPECTACULAR SIGHT
Although supernovae are fairly common in the universe, they are rarely seen from Earth. In 1987 a supernova was observed in the Large Magellanic Cloud, a nearby galaxy. The left-hand photograph shows the normal appearance of the star (arrowed). The supernova (designated SN 1987A) is clearly visible in the right-hand picture. After shining brightly for a few months, it slowly faded from view.

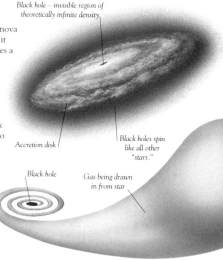

BLACK HOLES
If the core left after a supernova exceeds three solar masses, it will collapse until it becomes a black hole – something so dense that its gravity will suck in even light. By definition black holes are invisible, but they are believed to be surrounded by a spinning accretion disk of material being drawn into the black hole.

Black hole – invisible region of theoretically infinite density

Accretion disk

Black holes spin like all other "stars."

STELLAR THEFT
If a black hole forms near another star, it may suck in gas from the star, gradually stealing its mass. Astronomers believe that the object known as Cygnus X-1 is a star/black hole pair.

Black hole

Gas being drawn in from star

STELLAR CLASSIFICATION

THE MASS OF A STAR affects its other properties – its color, temperature, and luminosity. Each star is different, but by studying their properties, astronomers have been able to devise a system that enables them to classify all stars.

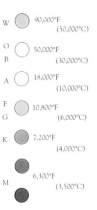

W	90,000°F (50,000°C)
O B	50,000°F (30,000°C)
A	18,000°F (10,000°C)
F G	10,800°F (6,000°C)
K	7,200°F (4,000°C)
M	6,300°F (3,500°C)

HEAT AND LIGHT

A star's color is usually a good indicator of its temperature. Blue stars are the hottest, and red the coolest. The Harvard system uses letters of the alphabet to classify stars according to their surface temperature. This diagram shows the color and temperature range of the main types.

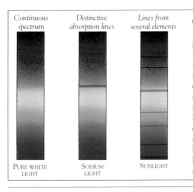

Continuous spectrum

Distinctive absorption lines

Lines from several elements

PURE WHITE LIGHT

SODIUM LIGHT

SUNLIGHT

CHEMICAL LINES

Each star emits its own particular light. Splitting this light into a spectrum reveals the chemical elements that make up the star. The different elements are indicated by dark absorption lines that run across the spectrum. Sodium atoms absorb light only in the yellow part of the spectrum. Sunlight displays hundreds of absorption lines, but only the most prominent are shown here.

HERTZSPRUNG-RUSSELL (HR) DIAGRAM OF STELLAR CLASSIFICATION

Supergiant stars e.g. Deneb

Betelgeuse is a red supergiant.

Main sequence stars, e.g. Sirius A, which convert hydrogen to helium

Arcturus is a red giant.

The Sun is a main sequence yellow dwarf.

White dwarf stars e.g. Sirius B

Barnard's Star is a main sequence red dwarf.

COLOR-CODED DIAGRAM

The HR diagram plots a star's temperature against its absolute magnitude (the amount of light it gives off). The brightest stars are at the top, and the dimmest are near the bottom. The hottest stars are to the left and the coolest to the right. Most stars spend some part of their lives in the main sequence which runs from top left to bottom right across the diagram. Giant stars are found above the main sequence and dwarf stars below.

STAR FACTS

• The hottest type W stars are very rare and are also known as Wolf-Rayet stars.

• By the standards of space, the Sun is very small. Astronomers refer to it as a type G dwarf star.

• Clusters of types O and B stars (known as OB1 clusters) contain hot, bright, young stars.

BRIGHTNESS

HOW BRIGHTLY A STAR shines in
the sky depends on its luminosity
(amount of light energy produced),
and on its distance from Earth.
Astronomers use two different
scales to measure a star's magnitude
(brightness). Absolute magnitude
compares stars from a standard
distance. Apparent magnitude
describes how bright a star appears
as viewed from Earth.

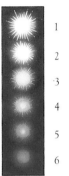

OBSERVED BRIGHTNESS
The scale of apparent
magnitude for naked-eye
stars. Brighter stars have
lower numerical values.

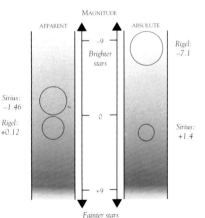

MAGNITUDE

APPARENT

ABSOLUTE

-9

*Brighter
stars*

Rigel:
-7.1

Sirius:
-1.46

Rigel:
+0.12

0

Sirius:
+1.4

+9

Fainter stars

APPARENT VS ABSOLUTE
Sirius is the brightest star
in our sky (apparent
magnitude -1.46) brighter
than Rigel (apparent
magnitude +0.12). Yet in
reality, Rigel is by far the
brighter star with an
absolute magnitude of
-7.1, as opposed to Sirius
which has an absolute
magnitude of +1.4.

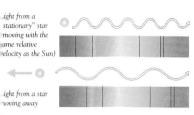

Light from a
"stationary" star
moving with the
same relative
velocity as the Sun

Light from a star
moving away

SHIFTING LIGHT

All objects in the universe are moving. In light from
stars moving away from the Sun, the dark absorption
lines are shifted toward the red end of the spectrum –
the so-called "red shift."

HOW FAR?

Calculating a star's absolute magnitude
means knowing its distance. For fairly
close stars (within a few hundred light-
years) astronomers can measure distance
using the parallax method. Earth's orbit
around the Sun enables astronomers to
take two sightings of a star from opposite
sides of the orbit. The apparent shift in
position of the star between the two
sightings is called the parallax.
The greater the parallax, the
nearer the star. In this case, star
A has the greater shift and
is the closer.

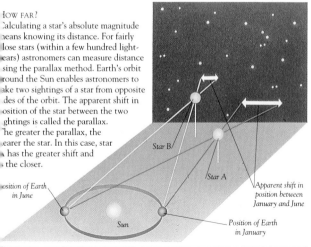

Star B

Star A

Apparent shift in
position between
January and June

Position of Earth
in June

Position of Earth
in January

Sun

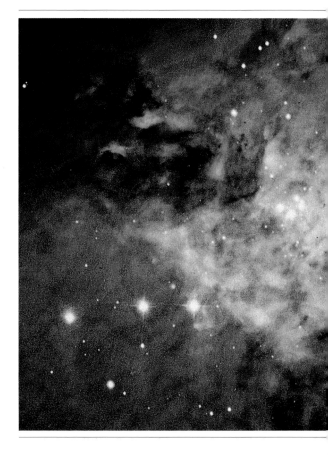

SPACE FROM EARTH

ABOVE OUR HEADS

OUR KNOWLEDGE of the universe has been gained from our unique position on Earth. By day the sky is dominated by the Sun. At night the blackness of space is studded with stars and galaxies which form an unchanging backdrop. However, our view of them changes throughout the year as Earth orbits the Sun.

CIRCULAR STAR TRAILS
Earth's daily rotation causes the stars to appear to circle around the sky. This effect can be captured by a long-exposure photograph.

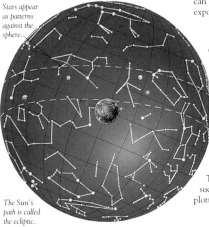

Stars appear as patterns against the sphere.

The Sun's path is called the ecliptic.

CELESTIAL SPHERE
From Earth the stars appear to be set against a giant celestial sphere. As the Earth travels on its yearly orbit around the Sun, different sections of the sphere are exposed to our view. At any particular time, about half the sphere is hidden by the Sun's glare. The motion of other objects such as the planets, are also plotted against the sphere.

GALAXY

All the stars we can see in the sky, including the Sun, are in the Milky Way galaxy. This panoramic view of the Milky Way (looking towards the centre of the galaxy), was photographed from Christchurch, New Zealand.

MARTIAN MOTION

Planets, which have their own orbits around the Sun, appear to move across the sky against the backdrop of stars. The name "planet" is in fact taken from an ancient Greek word meaning "wanderer." Of all the planets, Mars seems to wander the most – sometimes it appears to change direction and move backward across Earth's sky. This backward motion is in fact an optical illusion caused by the Earth overtaking Mars as it travels around the Sun.

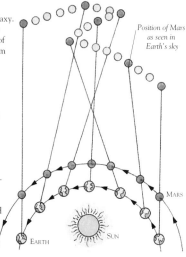

Position of Mars as seen in Earth's sky

EARTH

SUN

MARS

SPECIAL EFFECTS

FROM EARTH it is possible to see several "special effects" in the sky. Some of these effects are due to peculiarities of the Earth's magnetic field and atmosphere. Other effects depend on the position of the objects in the solar system, especially the Sun, Earth and Moon. Meteor showers are an effect produced by space dust burning up in the atmosphere.

AURORA BOREALIS
Charged particles from the Sun, carried by the solar wind, cause dramatic light shows when they enter Earth's atmosphere.

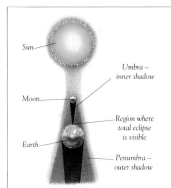

Sun

Umbra – inner shadow

Moon

Region where total eclipse is visible

Earth

Penumbra – outer shadow

ECLIPSE OF THE SUN
Occasionally, the Moon comes into perfect alignment between the Sun and the Earth. When this occurs, the Moon blocks out the Sun's light causing what is called a solar eclipse. From some parts of Earth's surface, the disc of the Moon appears to cover completely the Sun's face, and there is a brief period of darkness. Although the Moon is a great deal smaller than the Sun, it is able to block the light totally because it is so much nearer to the Earth.

HALO AROUND THE MOON

On some winter nights a halo appears around the Moon, but this has nothing to do with the Moon itself. Sunlight reflected toward Earth by the Moon is refracted (bent) by ice crystals high in Earth's atmosphere. This refraction of light creates a circular halo.

SPECIAL EFFECT FACTS

• Aurora borealis ("northern lights") are best observed from locations near the North Magnetic Pole. Similar displays in the Southern Hemisphere are called aurora australis.

• A lunar eclipse occurs when the Earth comes directly between the Sun and the Moon, and the Earth's shadow can be seen crossing the Moon's surface.

• A meteor radiant is an optical illusion. In fact, the meteors travel along parallel tracks.

METEOR RADIANT

Dust particles from space are seen as meteors when they burn up in the atmosphere. In a meteor shower, which is caused by dust from a comet, all the meteors appear to come from a single point in the sky. This point is known as the radiant of the meteor shower.

CONSTELLATIONS

SEEN FROM EARTH, the stars seem to form patterns in the sky. These patterns are known as constellations. The skies around Earth have been divided into 88 different constellations, each one of which is supposed to represent a mythological person, creature, or object.

CONSTELLATION OF ORION
In Greek myth, Orion was a mighty hunter. The three bright stars in a row form Orion's Belt, an easily located "skymark".

CELESTIAL SPHERE
AS SEEN FROM THE
NORTHERN HEMISPHERE

AROUND THE SPHERE
As the Earth makes its yearly orbit around the Sun, different portions of the celestial sphere come into view, presenting the constellations in an annual sequence.

Position of Earth in March

Constellations visible from Earth in March

100,000 YEARS AGO

TODAY

100,000 YEARS FROM NOW

CHANGING SHAPE
The constellations appear fixed, but
in fact they change very slowly. The
changes to the Big Dipper can only be
seen over very long periods of time.

LINES OF SIGHT
The constellations are a
human invention. We see them as
flat patterns against the blackness
of space, but in fact the stars may
be farther in distance from each
other than they are from
Earth. The stars in the Big
Dipper seem to be close
together. However,
they are more
scattered than
they appear.

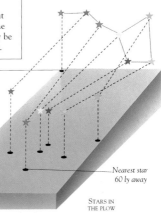

Farthest star
110 ly away

Nearest star
60 ly away

STARS IN
THE PLOW

CATALOGUING STARS

STARS ARE catalogued according
to the constellation in which
they appear. Within each
constellation, the individual
stars are identified by means of
letters or numbers. Other
objects are catalogued separately.

The constellation "figure" is drawn around the stars.

ORION

ORION NEBULA
In Earth's sky, the nebula
appears as a faint, fuzzy patch
of light just below Orion's Belt

POSSESSIVE NAMES
All the constellations have been
given Latin names. When referring to
a particular star, the possessive case of
the Latin name is used. For example,
stars in the constellation of Orion are
designated Orionis.

MAPPING THE SKIES
The constellations fit
together to map the sky.
All the stars inside
a constellation's
boundaries belong to
that constellation,
even if they appear
to be unconnected to
the star making up
the main "title" figure.

GALAXIES AND NEBULAE

Nonstellar objects, such as bright star clusters, nebulae, and other galaxies, are classified separately according to the Messier catalogue (numbers prefixed by letter M), or the New General Catalogue (numbers prefixed by the letters NGC).

GREEK LETTERS

The brighter stars in a constellation are identified by Greek letters. The brightest star is usually designated alpha (α), the next brightest beta (β) and so on, but this rule is not always followed.

Betelgeuse is catalogued as α Orionis.

Orion Nebula is catalogued as M42 and NGC1976.

Saiph is catalogued as κ Orionis.

Rigel is catalogued as β Orionis.

π_3 Orionis is 25 ly from Earth.

π_6 Orionis is 280 ly from Earth.

ARABIC NAMES

Many bright stars are still known by the individual names that were widely used by Arab astronomers more than 800 years ago – e.g. Betelgeuse. Saiph, and Rigel.

LETTERS AND NUMBERS

There are not enough letters in the Greek alphabet to label all the stars in constellations. Roman capital letters (A,B,C) and numbers (1,2,3) are also used. In some cases, Greek letters are used with subscript numbers to identify stars that are near to each other, for example π_3 and π_6 Orionis.

THE ZODIAC

TWELVE CONSTELLATIONS ARE known as the zodiac.
These twelve are crossed by the ecliptic (the Sun's
annual path around the celestial sphere), and form
the backdrop for the movement of the Moon and
planets. The Sun spends about a month passing
through each zodiac constellation. The dates usually
given for the zodiac are approximations – below are
the dates when the Sun actually enters each sign.

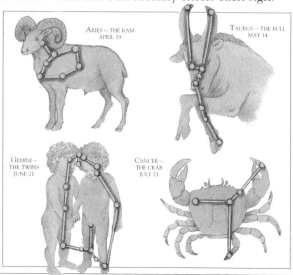

ARIES – THE RAM
APRIL 19

TAURUS – THE BULL
MAY 14

GEMINI –
THE TWINS
JUNE 21

CANCER –
THE CRAB
JULY 21

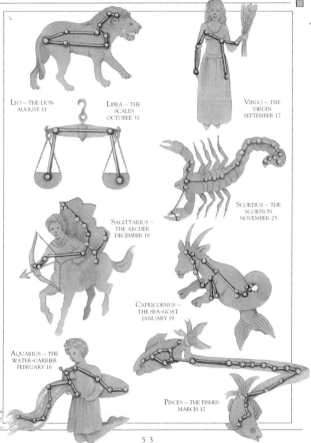

LEO – THE LION
AUGUST 11

LIBRA – THE
SCALES
OCTOBER 31

VIRGO – THE
VIRGIN
SEPTEMBER 17

SCORPIUS – THE
SCORPION
NOVEMBER 23

SAGITTARIUS –
THE ARCHER
DECEMBER 18

CAPRICORNUS –
THE SEA-GOAT
JANUARY 19

AQUARIUS – THE
WATER-CARRIER
FEBRUARY 16

PISCES – THE FISHES
MARCH 12

NEAR OR FAR?

STARS ARE VAST DISTANCES from
us and from each other. Light,
which travels faster than
anything else, takes 8.3 minutes
to travel from the Sun to the
Earth. Light from the next
nearest star, Proxima Centauri,
takes 4.3 years. People cannot
tell the distances to stars just by
looking at them. But they can
see subtle differences in color
and apparent brightness.

LIGHT-YEARS APART
All the stars in this distant
cluster may look as if they are
the same distance from Earth.
Yet in fact the stars are many
light-years apart.

HOW BRIGHT? HOW FAR?
Stars that have similar apparent magnitude
(brightness) can lie at hugely different
distances from Earth. Objects in the
constellation of Orion are between
70 and 2,300 light-years (ly)
from Earth. The brightest
star, Rigel, is more
than 900 ly away.

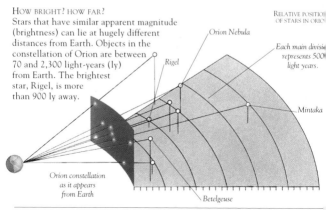

RELATIVE POSITION
OF STARS IN ORIO

Orion Nebula

Rigel

Each main divisi
represents 500
light-years.

Mintaka

Orion constellation
as it appears
from Earth

Betelgeuse

STELLAR DATA: NEAREST STARS TO THE SUN		
Name	Distance	Color
Proxima Centauri	4.2 ly	red
α Centauri A	4.3 ly	yellow
α Centauri B	4.3 ly	orange
Barnard's Star	5.9 ly	red
Wolf 359	7.6 ly	red
Lalande 21185	8.1 ly	red
Sirius A	8.6 ly	white
Sirius B	8.6 ly	white

STAR FACTS
• Proxima Centauri is part of a triple star system along with α Centauri A and α Centauri B.

• The brightest star, Sirius A, has a faint white dwarf companion, Sirius B.

NEIGHBORING STARS
Many of the stars within 40 light-years of the Sun are dim red dwarfs like Barnard's Star, which cannot be seen with the naked eye. Others, such as Vega, are 50 times more luminous than the Sun.

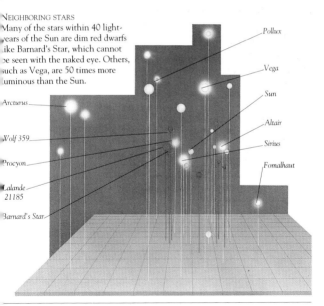

Pollux

Vega

Sun

Altair

Sirius

Fomalhaut

Arcturus

Wolf 359

Procyon

Lalande 21185

Barnard's Star

THE NORTHERN SKY

PEOPLE LIVING IN the Northern Hemisphere see the
northern half of the celestial sphere. The stars
visible on a particular night depend on the
observer's latitude, the time of year, and
the time of night. The stars near the center
of the sky-map are called circumpolar
and can be seen throughout the year.
Polaris (the North Star) appears to
remain directly over the North Pole.

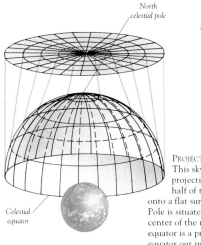

North celestial pole

Arcturus

Celestial equator

PROJECTED SPHERE
This sky-map is a
projection of the northern
half of the celestial sphere
onto a flat surface. Earth's North
Pole is situated directly below the
center of the map. The celestial
equator is a projection of Earth's
equator out into space.

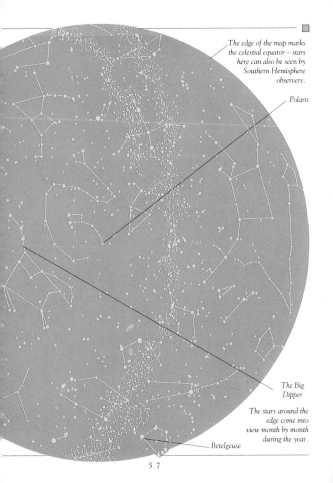

The edge of the map marks the celestial equator – stars here can also be seen by Southern Hemisphere observers.

Polaris

The Big Dipper

The stars around the edge come into view month by month during the year.

Betelgeuse

5 7

THE SOUTHERN SKY

PEOPLE LIVING IN the Southern Hemisphere see the
southern half of the celestial sphere. The stars
visible on a particular night depend on the
observer's latitude, the time of year, and
the time of night. The stars near the center
of the sky-map are called circumpolar
and can be seen all year round. Alpha
Centauri, one of the nearest stars to the
Sun, is a southern hemisphere star.

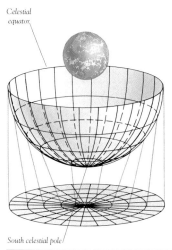

Celestial equator

Alpha Centauri

Antares

South celestial pole

PROJECTED SPHERE
This sky-map is a
projection of the
southern half of the
celestial sphere onto a
flat surface. Earth's South
Pole is situated directly
below the center of the
map. The celestial equator
is a projection of Earth's
equator out into space.

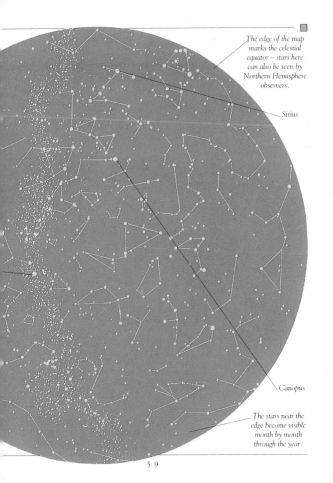

The edge of the map marks the celestial equator – stars here can also be seen by Northern Hemisphere observers.

Sirius

Canopus

The stars near the edge become visible month by month through the year.

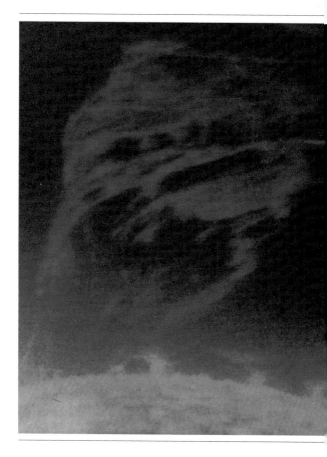

SOLAR
SYSTEM

WHAT IS THE SOLAR SYSTEM?

THE SOLAR SYSTEM consists of the Sun and the many objects that orbit around it – nine planets, over 60 moons, and countless asteroids and comets. The system occupies a disk-shaped volume of space more than 745 billion miles (1 billion kilometers) across. At the center is the Sun which contains more than 99 percent of the solar system's mass.

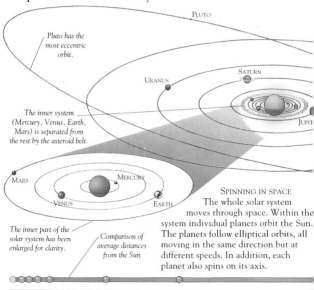

PLUTO

Pluto has the most eccentric orbit.

URANUS

SATURN

JUPIT

The inner system (Mercury, Venus, Earth, Mars) is separated from the rest by the asteroid belt.

MARS

MERCURY

VENUS

EARTH

The inner part of the solar system has been enlarged for clarity.

Comparison of average distances from the Sun

SPINNING IN SPACE
The whole solar system moves through space. Within the system individual planets orbit the Sun. The planets follow elliptical orbits, all moving in the same direction but at different speeds. In addition, each planet also spins on its axis.

MERCURY

VENUS

EARTH

MARS

Each of the four gas planets has a ring system around it – the rings have been omitted from this illustration for ease of comparison.

SOLAR SYSTEM FACTS

• Images obtained with the latest telescopes strongly suggest that some other stars (e.g. β Pictoris) are forming planetary systems.

• The solar system has a total of 61 moons by the latest count. Future space probes are almost certain to discover extra moons orbiting the outer planets.

JUPITER

Orbits are elliptical (oval) rather than circular

NEPTUNE

The time taken for a planet to make one orbit of the Sun is called the orbital period.

SATURN

URANUS

NEPTUNE

NINE PLANETS

The planets form two main groups – the inner four are composed of rock, while the next four are larger and are composed mostly of liquefied gas. The outermost planet, Pluto, is mainly rock.

PLUTO

Pluto is the smallest and least-known planet.

SOLAR GRAVITY

ABOUT 4.6 BILLION years ago, the solar system formed
from a cloud of gas and dust. The Sun formed first and
the other objects formed from
the leftovers. The Sun's
gravity dominates the
system because it is so
massive by comparison
with the planets.

CONDENSING INTO PLACE
The young Sun was surrounded
by a cloud of gas, snow,
and dust that flattened
into a disk. Dust clumped
together to form the four
inner rock planets. The
giant outer planets formed
from a mixture of gas, snow,
and dust. Pluto's origin is a mystery.

ORBITAL PATHS
Most of the planets orbit close to the plane of
the Earth's orbit (the ecliptic). Pluto has the
most inclined orbit, possibly because it is the
most distant planet and is the least influenced
by the Sun's gravity. However the next most
inclined planet is Mercury (7°),
which is the nearest
planet to the Sun.

THE PLANETS:
ORBITAL INCLINATION
TO THE ECLIPTIC

Pluto: 17.2°
Mercury: 7°
Venus: 3.39°
Saturn: 2.49°
Mars: 1.85°
Neptune: 1.77°
Jupiter: 1.3°
Uranus: 0.77°
Earth: 0°

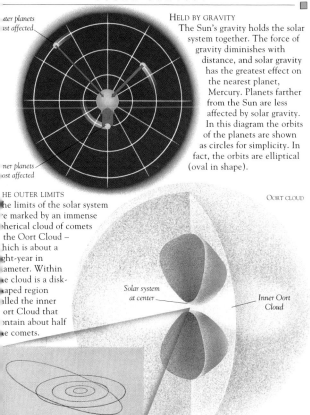

ter planets
st affected

ner planets
ost affected

HELD BY GRAVITY

The Sun's gravity holds the solar system together. The force of gravity diminishes with distance, and solar gravity has the greatest effect on the nearest planet, Mercury. Planets farther from the Sun are less affected by solar gravity. In this diagram the orbits of the planets are shown as circles for simplicity. In fact, the orbits are elliptical (oval in shape).

HE OUTER LIMITS

he limits of the solar system
e marked by an immense
pherical cloud of comets
the Oort Cloud –
hich is about a
ght-year in
ameter. Within
e cloud is a disk-
aped region
alled the inner
ort Cloud that
ontain about half
e comets.

OORT CLOUD

Solar system at center

Inner Oort Cloud

THE SUN

LIKE OTHER STARS, the Sun is
a huge ball of spinning gas.
Nuclear reactions take place
at its core, giving off energy.
The Sun is the only star close
enough to be studied in detail.
Its surface features, such as
sunspots and prominences,
can be observed from Earth.
Satellites and space probes are
able to get a closer view and
obtain even more information.

ECLIPSE OF THE SUN
During an eclipse, the outer
layer of the Sun, the corona,
becomes visible. Normally
the corona is hidden by glare.

Year 1   Year 4   Year 7   Year 10   Year 12

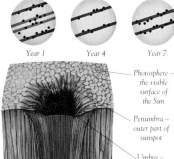

Photosphere –
the visible
surface of
the Sun

Penumbra –
outer part of
sunspot

Umbra –
coolest and
darkest part

COOL AND DARK
Sunspots, dark patches on the
surface, are regions of cooler gas
caused by disturbances in the
Sun's magnetic field. Sunspots
follow an 11-year cycle that
begins with the Sun being spot-
free. The spots appear at high
latitude and gradually increase
in number, moving toward the
Sun's equator during the cycle.

SOLAR DATA

Average distance from Earth	93,026,724 miles (149,680,000 km)
Distance from center of galaxy	30,000 light-years
Diameter (at equator)	865,121 miles (1,391,980 km)
Rotation period (at equator)	25.04 Earth days
Mass (Earth = 1)	330,000
Gravity (Earth = 1)	27.9
Average density (water = 1)	1.41
Absolute magnitude	4.83

SOLAR FACTS

• Never look directly at the Sun. Even with sunglasses, camera film, or smoked glass you risk damaging your eyesight.

• The safe way is to project the Sun's image onto a piece of paper using a hand lens.

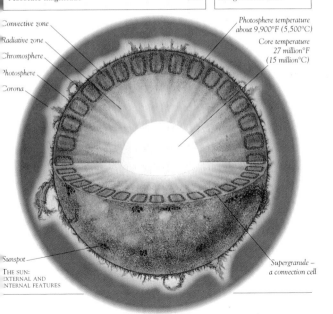

Convective zone
Radiative zone
Chromosphere
Photosphere
Corona

Photosphere temperature about 9,900°F (5,500°C)
Core temperature 27 million°F (15 million°C)

Sunspot

THE SUN: EXTERNAL AND INTERNAL FEATURES

Supergranule – a convection cell

SOLAR ENERGY AND INFLUENCE

AT ITS CORE, the Sun converts hydrogen to helium at a rate of 600 million tons (tonnes) every second. The energy produced eventually reaches the surface and travels through space.

Visible light and other radiation travels from the Sun's surface to Earth in about 8 minutes.

Nuclear reactions at core produce gamma rays

Gamma rays take up to two million years to travel to surface, losing energy in the process

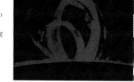

SOLAR PROMINENCES
Enormous jets of hot gas shoot out from the Sun's surface stretching for many thousands of miles (kilometers). The largest jets, called prominences, can last for several months. The Sun's magnetic field holds some prominences in gigantic loops.

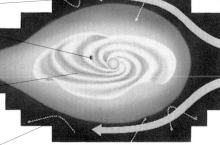

Solar wind deflects interstellar gas

The solar wind takes about five days to reach Earth.

Around Earth the solar wind blows at about 311 miles/sec (500 km/s).

Solar wind deflects most cosmic rays

ULYSSES
SOLAR PROBE

Sensors located on hinged boom

EXTENT OF INFLUENCE

The Sun influences an enormous volume of space around it. Gases streaming from the corona become the high-speed solar wind. The solar wind carries a magnetic field from the Sun. As the Sun rotates, the field takes on a spiral shape. The volume of space swept by the solar wind is called the heliosphere.

TO THE SOLAR POLES

Earth's orbit in the Sun's equatorial plane means that the Sun's poles cannot be studied from Earth. The Ulysses probe was launched in 1990 to study these hard-to-observe regions.

SOLAR ENERGY FACTS

• Converting hydrogen to helium means that the Sun loses four million tons (tonnes) of its mass every second.

• The amount of the Sun's energy reaching Earth's surface (known as the solar constant) is equivalent to 1.37 kw (kilowatts) of electricity per square yard (meter) per second.

PLANETS

MERCURY

A SMALL ROCK WORLD with a
large dense core, Mercury is
the closest planet to the Sun.
There is no real atmosphere,
and much of the surface is
marked by numerous impact
craters. Dominated by the
Sun, Mercury experiences the
greatest variation in surface
temperature of any planet in
the solar system. Differences
between day and night can be
more than 1,080°F (600°C).

DIFFICULT TO SEE
Photographs taken from Earth
show Mercury as a fuzzy disk,
difficult to observe against the
Sun. This image was put
together from photographs
taken by the Mariner 10 probe.

Earth

Mercury

MERCURY: PLANETARY DATA	
Average distance from the Sun	36 million miles (57.9 million km)
Orbital period	88 Earth days
Orbital velocity	29.7 miles/sec (47.9 km/s)
Rotation period	58.7 Earth days
Diameter at equator	3,032 miles (4,878 km)
Surface temperature	−292°F to +806°F (−180°C to +430°C)
Mass (Earth = 1)	0.055
Gravity (Earth = 1)	0.38
Number of moons	0

MERCURY FACTS
• Mercury was named
after the fleet-footed
messenger of the
Roman gods because it
travels so quickly across
Earth's sky.

• Mercury's largest
crater, Caloris Planitia,
measures 875 miles
(1,400 km) across.

56% oxygen

35% sodium

8% helium

1% potassium and hydrogen

MERCURY:
COMPOSITION OF ATMOSPHERE

THIN AIR
Mercury's atmosphere is
extremely thin – less
than one trillionth of
Earth's. Sodium and
potassium occur in the
daytime only. At night
these elements are
absorbed back into the
surface rocks.

PROBE'S EYE VIEW
Craters cover about 60
percent of Mercury's surface.
The other 40 percent consists
of relatively smooth plains.

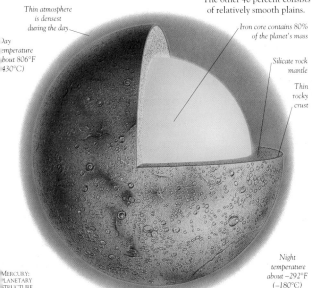

*Thin atmosphere
is densest
during the day*

*Day
temperature
about 806°F
(430°C)*

*Iron core contains 80%
of the planet's mass*

*Silicate rock
mantle*

*Thin
rocky
crust*

MERCURY:
PLANETARY
STRUCTURE

*Night
temperature
about −292°F
(−180°C)*

LONG DAYS

Mercury rotates very slowly on an almost upright axis. The axis is tilted at just 2° from the normal (at 90°) to the plane of its orbit. A single day on Mercury (sunrise to sunrise) lasts for 176 Earth days. Although days are very long, the Mercurian year is very short. The planet takes only 88 Earth days to complete one orbit around the Sun.

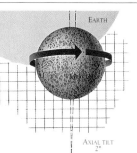

EARTH

MERCURY

AXIAL TILT
2°

ECCENTRIC ORBIT

A combination of long days and short years would create strange effects for any inhabitants. While Mercury completes two orbits of the Sun (shown here separately for clarity), an observer on the surface (marked by a dot) would experience only one Mercurian day. Birthdays would happen more often than sunrise.

SURFACE MAP

The Mariner 10 photographs were used to produce maps of Mercury. Each square of the grid covers about 50 x 50 miles (80 x 80 km).

IMPACT CRATER FORMATION ON ROCK PLANETS

A meteorite impact blasts out a circular crater, and ejected material falls back to form a circular rim.

Rock compressed by the initial impact may bounce back from the sides to form a roughly conical central peak.

The crater profile is gradually reduced as rock fragments and debris slip from the walls and peak.

SOLITARY VISITOR

Mariner 10 is the only probe to have made a detailed study of Mercury. Launched in November 1973, the probe took five months to reach the planet. During three close approaches the probe photographed about 40 percent of the surface area. At its closest approach, Mariner 10 was 187 miles (300 km) above the surface.

High resolution cameras

MARINER 10 PROBE

MERCURY: CREATIVE CRATER NAMES

Mercury's craters commemorate creative people:

Writers	Composers	Painters	Architects
Bronte	Bach	Brueghel	Bernini
Cervantes	Chopin	Cezanne	Bramante
Dickens	Grieg	Dürer	Imhotep
Goethe	Handel	Holbein	Mansart
Li Po	Liszt	Monet	Michelangelo
Melville	Mozart	Renoir	Sinan
Shelley	Stravinsky	Titian	Sullivan
Tolstoy	Verdi	Van Gogh	Wren

FACTS

• Mercury can only be seen from Earth at twilight – either just before dawn or just after sunset.

• Parts of Mercury's surface have a wrinkled appearance – the result of the planet shrinking as its core cooled.

VENUS

A ROCK PLANET with a dense
atmosphere, Venus is almost
the same size as the Earth.
The two share some surface
features, but conditions on
Venus are very different from
those on Earth. The surface
environment of Venus is
extremely hostile – intense
heat, crushing pressure, and
unbreathable air. Overhead
there are thick clouds of
sulfuric acid droplets.

OBSCURED BY CLOUDS
The surface features of Venus
are hidden by a permanent
blanket of thick cloud. The
dark swirls are high-altitude
wind systems.

Venus

Earth

VENUS: PLANETARY DATA	
Average distance from the Sun	67.2 million miles (108.2 million km)
Orbital period	224.7 Earth days
Orbital velocity	21.7 miles/sec (35 km/s)
Rotation period	243 Earth days
Diameter at equator	7,521 miles (12,102 km)
Surface temperature	896°F (480°C)
Mass (Earth = 1)	0.81
Gravity (Earth = 1)	0.88
Number of moons	0

VENUS FACTS

• Venus shines brightly
in Earth's sky because
the cloud layer reflects
most of the sunlight.

• Venus has phases like
the Moon. You need a
telescope to see them
clearly, but binoculars
will enable you to see
the crescent phase.

Upper haze

*Cloud layer
12.5 miles
(20 km)
thick*

Lower haze

ⁱENUS: ATMOSPHERE
ⁱTRUCTURE AND COMPOSITION

BENEATH THE CLOUDS
Below the clouds is a clear
carbon-dioxide atmosphere.
At the surface, atmospheric
pressure is 90 times that of
Earth at sea level.

96% carbon dioxide

	3.5% nitrogen

	0.5% sulfur dioxide, argon, and carbon monoxide

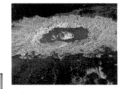

COMPUTER IMAGE
This is a computer-generated
image of the Howe meteorite
crater 23 miles (37 km) in
diameter. The image was
produced from radar-
mapping data.

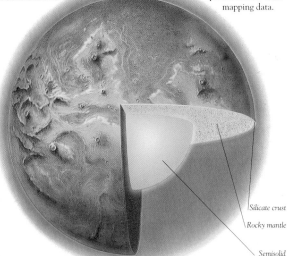

Silicate crust

Rocky mantle

Semisolid
iron-nickel core

BACKWARD ROTATION

Venus is one of only two planets to rotate on its axis in a backward direction (the other is remote Pluto). Venus' backward rotation is so slow that a Venusian day lasts longer (243 Earth days) than a Venusian year (224.7 Earth days). Driven by powerful winds, Venus' atmosphere moves at its own, much faster, pace. The upper levels of the cloud layer take just four Earth days to travel right around the planet.

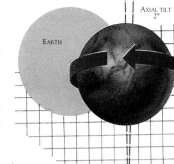

AXIAL TILT
2°

EARTH

62 miles
(100 km)

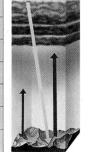

Sunlight reflected by cloud layer

GREENHOUSE PLANET

Venus has a higher average surface temperature (896°F -480°C) than any other planet in the solar system. The heating of Venus is the result of a "greenhouse effect" run wild. Although the cloud layer reflects much of the sunlight that hits it, some solar heat energy does reach the surface. But instead of being radiated back into space, this heat energy is trapped by the cloud layer causing temperatures to rise. On Earth the cloud layer allows much more heat to escape.

EARTH

VENUS

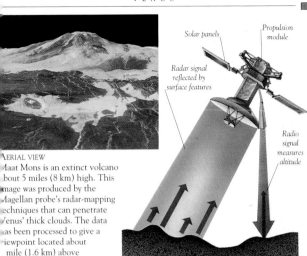

AERIAL VIEW

Maat Mons is an extinct volcano about 5 miles (8 km) high. This image was produced by the Magellan probe's radar-mapping techniques that can penetrate Venus' thick clouds. The data has been processed to give a viewpoint located about 1 mile (1.6 km) above the planet's surface.

Solar panels

Propulsion module

Radar signal reflected by surface features

Radio signal measures altitude

VENUS: SELECTED EXPLORATION EVENTS		
Probe	Date	Result
Mariner 2	14/12/62	Successful flyby
Venera 4	18/10/67	Sampled atmosphere
Venera 7	15/12/70	Sent data from surface
Mariner 10	5/2/74	Flyby on way to Mercury
Venera 9	23/10/75	First orbit and soft landing and first surface image
Venera 15	10/10/83	First radar mapping
Pioneer-Venus 2	9/12/78	Multiple descent probes investigate atmosphere
Magellan	10/8/90	Complete radar mapping

MORE FACTS

• The facts that Venus has a small axial tilt and backward rotation is just popular convention. According to the rules of the IAU (International Astronomical Union), Venus rotates in a normal direction around an axis tilted at 177.9° to the vertical.

EARTH

THE THIRD PLANET from the
Sun, Earth, is unique in the
solar system and is possibly
unique in the universe.
Only Earth has the range of
temperatures that permit
liquid water to exist, and
Earth alone has developed
an oxygen-rich atmosphere.
These two factors have
enabled the rocky planet
Earth to evolve myriad
varieties of life.

JEWEL IN SPACE
Photographed by Apollo
astronauts returning from the
Moon, planet Earth looks like a
brightly colored jewel – blue
oceans, white clouds, and green-
brown land masses.

Earth

EARTH: PLANETARY DATA	
Average distance from the Sun	93 million miles (149.6 million km)
Orbital period	365.25 days
Orbital velocity	18.5 miles/sec (29.8 km/s)
Rotation period	23.93 hours
Diameter at equator	7,928 miles (12,756 km)
Surface temperature	–94°F to +131°F (–55°C to +70°C)
Gravity (Earth = 1)	1
Number of moons	1

EARTH FACTS
• The oldest rocks so
far discovered in the
Earth's crust date back
3.9 billion years.
• The oxygen in
Earth's atmosphere is
the result of life. The
process of oxygenation
began with bacteria
about 2 billion years
ago.

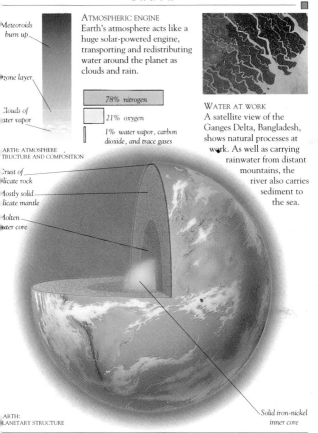

ATMOSPHERIC ENGINE
Earth's atmosphere acts like a huge solar-powered engine, transporting and redistributing water around the planet as clouds and rain.

78% nitrogen
21% oxygen
1% water vapor, carbon dioxide, and trace gases

WATER AT WORK
A satellite view of the Ganges Delta, Bangladesh, shows natural processes at work. As well as carrying rainwater from distant mountains, the river also carries sediment to the sea.

Meteoroids burn up
Ozone layer
Clouds of water vapor
EARTH: ATMOSPHERE STRUCTURE AND COMPOSITION

Crust of silicate rock
Mostly solid silicate mantle
Molten outer core
EARTH: PLANETARY STRUCTURE

Solid iron-nickel inner core

UNEQUAL HEATING

Earth's axis of rotation is tilted at 23.5° to the vertical. As the planet travels around the Sun during the year, the tilt causes seasonal variations in climate. These variations are most noticeable in the high latitudes away from the equator. Spinning on a tilted axis gives rise to unequal heating of the surface by the Sun. This differential heating produces differences in atmospheric pressure which create the wind systems that drive Earth's climate.

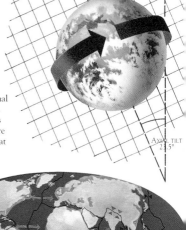

AXIAL TILT 23.5°

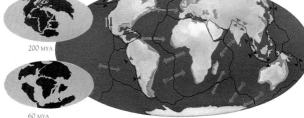

200 MYA

60 MYA

200 MILLION YEARS AGO
The continents were grouped closer together.

60 MILLION YEARS AGO
The landmasses had moved some way towards their present locations.

CONTINENTS IN MOTION

The continents "float" on the surface of the Earth's crust, which is made up of a number of separate plates. These plates are in constant slow-motion, pushed apart as new crust is produced at mid-ocean ridges. The result is that the continents are also gradually moving. Areas where plates are in collision have many volcanoes and earthquakes.

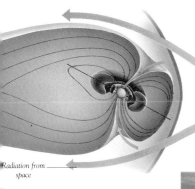

SPINNING MAGNET
Earth has a much stronger magnetic field than any of the other rock planets. Produced by the rapid rotation of the nickel-iron core, the magnetic field extends far into space and deflects harmful radiation away from the planet. Despite its elongated ovoid shape, this magnetic field is called the magnetosphere.

Radiation from space

THE WATER OF LIFE
Water only exists in its liquid form between 2°F (0°C) and 212°F (100°C), which is about the same range of temperatures found on Earth. Liquid water is absolutely essential to practically all forms of life. Along with carbon dioxide, it is one of the two raw materials used by plants to produce their own food and provide the oxygen upon which animal life depends.

EARTH: PHYSICAL LIMITS

Age	4.6 billion years
Mass	59,760 trillion tons (tonnes)
Surface area	317 million sq miles
	(510 million km²)
Covered by water	70.8 percent
Highest mountain	510 million km²
	(8,848 meters)
Deepest ocean trench	35,800 ft (10,924 meters)
Oldest evidence of life	3.5 billion years ago

MORE FACTS
• The Atlantic Ocean increases in width by about 1.2 in (3 cm) each year.
• Earth has periodic magnetic reversals when the north pole becomes the south pole, and the south becomes north.

EARTH'S MOON

EARTH HAS A single satellite, the Moon, which is about one-quarter the size of our planet. Although the Earth and the Moon are closely linked, there are many striking contrasts. The Moon is a waterless, airless, and lifeless place. Its surface is covered by craters, the scars of a massive meteorite bombardment that took place billions of years ago.

FAMILIAR SIGHT
Some of the features on the Moon can be identified with the naked eye. Binoculars, or a small telescope, will reveal a considerable amount of detail.

The Moon's distance from Earth varies during its orbit.

Minimum   Average   Maximum

THE MOON: DATA	
Average distance from the Earth	238,970 miles (384,500 km)
Orbital period	27.3 Earth days
Orbital velocity	0.6 miles/sec (1 km/s)
Rotation period	27.3 Earth days
Diameter at equator	2,160 miles (3,476 km)
Surface temperature	–247°F to +221°F (–155°C to +105°C)
Mass (Earth = 1)	0.012
Gravity (Earth = 1)	0.16
Escape velocity	1.48 miles/sec (2.38 km/s)

MOON FACTS
• The Moon has approximately the same surface area as the continents of North and South America.

• The pull of the Moon's gravity is largely responsible for the twice daily rise and fall of tides in Earth's seas and oceans.

FIGURE IN A MOONSCAPE
The Moon remains unique as the only
extraterrestrial object upon which
human beings have walked. Protected
by a spacesuit from the airless lunar
environment, one of the Apollo 17
astronauts investigates a large boulder.
Undisturbed by the effects of wind or
rain, his footprints should remain
visible for millions of years.

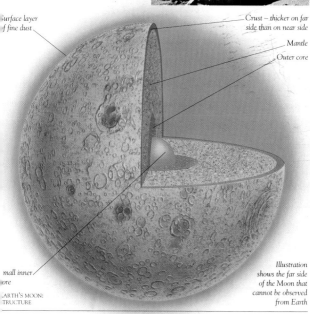

Surface layer
of fine dust

Crust – thicker on far
side than on near side

Mantle

Outer core

Small inner
core

EARTH'S MOON:
STRUCTURE

Illustration
shows the far side
of the Moon that
cannot be observed
from Earth

HELD IN PLACE

Earth is larger and more massive than the Moon, and has a powerful effect on its smaller neighbor. Under the influence of Earth's gravity the Moon's motion through space has been moderated so that its rotation period is the same as its orbital period – 27.3 days. This synchronization of motion means that the same face of the Moon is always turned toward the Earth – the near side. The other side is always turned away from us – the far side.

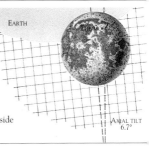

EARTH

THE MOON

AXIAL TILT 6.7°

BATTERED SURFACE

About 3.8 billion years ago, the Moon's surface received an intense meteorite bombardment.

Some 1 billion years later, the largest craters gradually filled up with dark lava, and formed the lunar seas.

Since that time, the appearance of the lunar surface has hardly changed apart from a few recent ray craters.

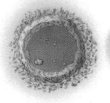

OLD CRATER

RAY CRATER

CHANGING MOONSCAPE

Most of the craters were made about 3 billion years ago, and many are only faintly visible. Some newer craters are identifiable by conspicuous rays of pale ejected material fanning out from the crater wall.

MOON ROCK

About 836 lb (380 kg) of moon rock have been brought back to Earth. There are no sedimentary or metamorphic rocks on the Moon – all the samples brought back are either igneous lavas (mainly basalt) or breccias produced by the heat and force of meteorite impacts. Most of the Moon's surface is covered with a layer of crushed and broken rock (called "regolith") which is about 65 ft (20 m) deep .

MOON ROCK COLLECTED BY APOLLO ASTRONAUTS

PHASES OF THE MOON

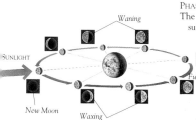

Waning

SUNLIGHT

New Moon

Waxing

Full Moon

The Moon shines by reflected sunlight. As it travels around the Earth, the visible amount of sunlit area changes day by day. Viewed from Earth's surface, this produces a cycle of lunar phases – waxing from New Moon to Full Moon, and then waning back to New Moon once more.

EARTH'S MOON: SELECTED EXPLORATION EVENTS		
Vehicle	Date	Result
Luna 3	10/10/59	First images of far side
Luna 9	3/2/66	First soft landing
Surveyor 3	17/4/67	Landing site soil studies
Apollo 11	20/7/69	Humans first land on Moon
Luna 16	24/9/70	Robot returns with samples
Luna 17	17/11/70	Mobile robot landed
Apollo 15	30/7/71	Lunar Roving Vehicle used
Apollo 17	11/12/72	Last Apollo mission lands

MORE FACTS

• The first person to step on to the Moon was the astronaut Neil Armstrong early on July 21, 1969.

• His historic first words were, " That's one small step for man, one giant leap for mankind."

MARS

A RED-HUED ROCKY PLANET,
Mars is a cold, barren world
with a thin atmosphere. There
are many Earthlike features,
such as polar ice caps and water-
carved valleys, but there are
many important differences.
Temperatures rarely rise above
the freezing point, the air is
unbreathable, and dust-storms
occasionally scour the surface.
The planet's red color is caused
by the presence of iron oxide.

LONG RANGE VIEW
This image was obtained by an
Earth-orbiting telescope at a
distance of 53 million miles
(85 million km) from Mars.
Bluish clouds can be seen
above the north pole region.

Earth

Mars

MARS: PLANETARY DATA	
Average distance from the Sun	141.6 million miles (227.9 million km)
Orbital period	687 Earth days
Orbital velocity	15 miles/sec (24.1 km/s)
Rotation period	24.62 hours
Diameter at equator	4,217 miles (6,786 km)
Surface temperature	–184°F to +77°F (–120°C to +25°C)
Mass (Earth = 1)	0.107
Gravity (Earth = 1)	0.38
Moons:	2

MARS FACTS
• Mars was named
after the Roman god
of war because it
appears the color of
spilled blood.
• The south polar ice
cap on Mars is much
larger than the north
polar ice cap, and the
southern winter is
considerably longer.

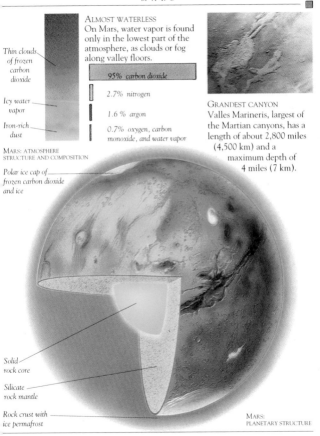

Thin clouds of frozen carbon dioxide

Icy water vapor

Iron-rich dust

MARS: ATMOSPHERE STRUCTURE AND COMPOSITION

ALMOST WATERLESS
On Mars, water vapor is found only in the lowest part of the atmosphere, as clouds or fog along valley floors.

95% carbon dioxide

2.7% nitrogen

1.6 % argon

0.7% oxygen, carbon monoxide, and water vapor

GRANDEST CANYON
Valles Marineris, largest of the Martian canyons, has a length of about 2,800 miles (4,500 km) and a maximum depth of 4 miles (7 km).

Polar ice cap of frozen carbon dioxide and ice

Solid rock core

Silicate rock mantle

Rock crust with ice permafrost

MARS: PLANETARY STRUCTURE

EARTHLIKE SEASONS
Mars is smaller than
the Earth, but turns
on its axis more
slowly, so that the
day lengths are almost
identical. A day on
Mars is just 41 minutes
longer. A similar axial
tilt gives Mars the same
pattern of seasons as we
experience on Earth. However,
because of the greater orbital
period (687 Earth days), the length
of each season is nearly twice as long.

EARTH

AXIAL TILT
25.2°

DESERT SURFACE
This is a view of the Martian surface
photographed by the Viking I lander.
Part of the lander is seen here in the
foreground. The rocks in the middle of
the picture are about 1 ft (30 cm) across,
and this "stony desert" appearance is
typical of about 40 percent of Mars'
surface area. Some Martian landforms,
however, are more dramatic. Olympus
Mons towers 15.5 miles (25 km) high.

*Olympus Mons, a giant
shield volcano, is the tallest
mountain in the
solar system.*

*Earth's Mauna Kea volcano is
dwarfed by comparison.*

Hawaiian Islands   *Ocean floor*   *Sea level*

ORBITS OF MARS' MOONS

Deimos

Phobos

SCALE IN RADIUSES OF MARS

8   7   6   5   4   3   2   1

SMALL MOONS

Mars has two tiny moons, Phobos and Deimos, neither of them more than 18.5 miles (30 km) in length. Both are irregularly shaped and have every appearance of being asteroids that were captured by Mars' gravity. Phobos orbits Mars at a distance of 5,830 miles (9,380 km) every 7 hours and 40 minutes. Deimos orbits three times farther away, at a distance of 14,581 miles (23,462 km), and takes about 30 hours to circle the planet.

Smaller and darker than its companion

DEIMOS

PHOBOS

The crater Stickney is nearly 6.2 miles (10 km) across

MARS: SELECTED EXPLORATION EVENTS		
Vehicle	Date	Result
Mariner 4	7/14/65	First fly-by images
Mars 3	12/2/71	Orbit achieved, lander failed after 20 seconds
Mariner 9	11/13/71	Photomapped surface from Martian orbit
Viking 1 and	7/20/76	Successful soft landings provide images and soil data
Viking 2	9/3/76	but no evidence of life

MORE FACTS

• Phobos means "fear," and Deimos means "terror" – suitable companions for the planet named after a god of war.

• Viewed from the surface of Mars, Phobos crosses the sky three times each day.

JUPITER

THE LARGEST of the planets,
Jupiter has two and a half
times more mass than all
the other planets together.
Jupiter has a small rock
core, but consists mainly of
gas in various physical
states. The mantle of cold
liquefied gas merges into a
dense atmosphere. Giant
wind systems give Jupiter a
banded appearance.

GAS GIANT
Voyager I photographed Jupiter
from a distance of 17.5 million
miles (28.4 million km). The moon
Io is just visible against a background
of Jupiter's stormy atmosphere.

Earth   Jupiter

JUPITER: PLANETARY DATA	
Average distance from the Sun	483.7 million miles (778.3 million km)
Orbital period	11.86 Earth years
Orbital velocity	8.1 miles/sec (13.1 km/s)
Rotation period	9.84 hours
Diameter at equator	88,865 miles (142,984 km)
Cloud-top temperature	–238°F (–150°C)
Mass (Earth = 1)	318
Gravity (Earth = 1)	2.54
Number of moons	16

JUPITER FACTS

• The pressure in
Jupiter's interior is so
great that hydrogen
gas exists naturally in
a semisolid metallic
form not yet made
on Earth.

• Jupiter can be seen
with the naked eye as
a bright silver "star"
in Earth's night sky.

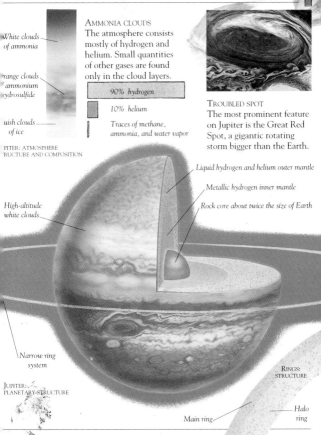

White clouds
of ammonia

range clouds
ammonium
ydrosulfide

uish clouds
of ice

PITER: ATMOSPHERE
RUCTURE AND COMPOSITION

AMMONIA CLOUDS
The atmosphere consists
mostly of hydrogen and
helium. Small quantities
of other gases are found
only in the cloud layers.

| 90% hydrogen |
| 10% helium |
| Traces of methane, ammonia, and water vapor |

TROUBLED SPOT
The most prominent feature
on Jupiter is the Great Red
Spot, a gigantic rotating
storm bigger than the Earth.

Liquid hydrogen and helium outer mantle

Metallic hydrogen inner mantle

Rock core about twice the size of Earth

High-altitude
white clouds

Narrow ring
system

JUPITER:
PLANETARY-STRUCTURE

RINGS:
STRUCTURE

Main ring

Halo
ring

9 3

FASTEST SPINNER

Despite its enormous size, 11 times the diameter of Earth, Jupiter rotates on its axis faster than any other planet. This high-speed rotation causes the gas giant to bulge around the equator, giving it a slightly oval shape. The rapid rotation also produces the powerful wind systems which divide Jupiter's atmosphere into bands that lie parallel with the equator. The most powerful winds move at speeds of several hundred miles (kilometers) per hour.

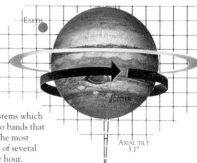

EARTH

JUPITER

AXIAL TILT 3.1°

THE GALILEAN MOONS:

EUROPA
Covered by a smooth layer of solid ice, Europa has sufficient internal heat to have seas of liquid water lying beneath its featureless surface.

CALLISTO
Covered with cracked and dirty ice around a rock core, Callisto is scarred by many craters. The largest is named Valhalla, with a diameter of 1,865 miles (3,000 km).

GANYMEDE
The largest moon in the solar system, Ganymede is larger than the planets Pluto and Mercury. Believed to consist mainly of ice and slush, Ganymede may have a silicate rock core.

IO

Debris from many volcanoes gives Io's surface an orange color. The interior is still molten, and Io has the first active volcanoes to be discovered outside the Earth.

MOONS OF JUPITER

The four largest moons were discovered by Galileo, hence their collective name. The others have been discovered subsequently, some of them by the Voyager I probe. The four outermost moons orbit in the opposite direction to all the other moons.

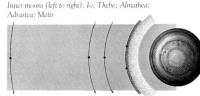

Inner moons (left to right): Io; Thebe; Almathea; Adrastea; Metis

Outer moons (left to right): Sinope; Pasiphae; Carme; Ananke; Elara; Lysithea; Himalia; Leda; Callisto; Ganymede; Europa; Io (also shown above)

SCALE IN RADIUSES OF JUPITER

JUPITER: SATELLITE DATA

	Diameter		Distance from Jupiter	
	miles	km	miles	km
Metis	25	40	79,528	127,960
Adrastea	12.5	20	80,162	128,980
Almathea	124	200	112,679	181,300
Thebe	62	100	137,912	221,900
Io	2,256	3,630	262,026	421,600
Europa	1,950	3,138	416,967	670,900
Ganymede	3,270	5,262	665,009	1,070,000
Callisto	2,983	4,800	1,170,292	1,883,000
Leda	10	16	6,894,966	11,094,000
Himalia	112	180	7,134,866	11,480,000
Lysithea	25	40	7,284,027	11,720,000
Elara	50	80	7,294,592	11,737,000
Ananke	19	30	13,175,885	21,200,000
Carme	27	44	14,045,991	22,600,000
Pasiphae	43	70	14,605,344	23,500,000
Sinope	25	40	14,729,645	23,700,000

MORE FACTS

• The orbital periods of planetary satellites increase according to their distance from the planet. Innermost Metis orbits Jupiter in 0.295 Earth days, while Sinope takes 758 days.

• The Voyager probes obtained 30,000 images of Jupiter and its moons.

• The volcanoes on Io eject material at speeds up to 3,285 ft per sec (1,000 m/s). This is about 20 times faster than material from volcanoes on Earth.

SATURN

FAMED FOR ITS magnificent
ring system, Saturn is the
second largest of the planets.
Like its nearest neighbor
Jupiter, Saturn is a gas
giant. However, the mass
is so spread out that on
average the planet is less
dense than water. Saturn has
more moons than any other
planet – at least 18. The
largest moon, Titan, has an
unusually thick atmosphere.

RINGED WORLD
Saturn is at the limit of easy
telescopic viewing from
Earth. This photograph was
taken at a distance of
11 million miles (17.5 million
km) by Voyager 2.

Earth   *Saturn*

SATURN: PLANETARY DATA

Average distance from the Sun:	886.9 million miles 1,427 million km
Orbital period	29.46 Earth years
Orbital velocity	6 miles/sec (9.6 km/s)
Rotation period	10.23 hours
Diameter at equator	74,914 miles (120,536 km)
Cloud-top temperature	–292°F (–180°C)
Mass (Earth = 1)	95
Gravity (Earth = 1)	0.93
Number of moons	18

SATURN FACTS
• Saturn's rings are less
than 656 ft (200 m)
thick, but over 167,800
miles (270,000 km) in
diameter.

• The rings consist
of billions of ice-
covered rock
fragments and
dust particles.

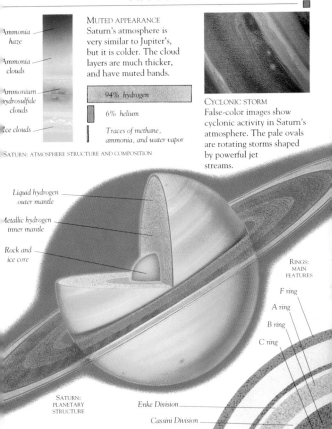

MUTED APPEARANCE
Saturn's atmosphere is
very similar to Jupiter's,
but it is colder. The cloud
layers are much thicker,
and have muted bands.

Ammonia
haze

Ammonia
clouds

Ammonium
hydrosulfide
clouds

Ice clouds

94% hydrogen

6% helium

Traces of methane,
ammonia, and water vapor

SATURN: ATMOSPHERE STRUCTURE AND COMPOSITION

CYCLONIC STORM
False-color images show
cyclonic activity in Saturn's
atmosphere. The pale ovals
are rotating storms shaped
by powerful jet
streams.

Liquid hydrogen
outer mantle

Metallic hydrogen
inner mantle

Rock and
ice core

RINGS:
MAIN
FEATURES

F ring

A ring

B ring

C ring

SATURN:
PLANETARY
STRUCTURE

Enke Division

Cassini Division

TILTED SYSTEM

Saturn rotates very rapidly on an axis that is tilted at 26.7° to the vertical. The orbits of the rings and moons are all aligned with this rotation, and lie in the same plane as the planet's equator, giving the whole system a tilted appearance. Like the other giant gas planets, Saturn bulges noticeably at the equator where the speed of rotation is faster than at the poles. Inside the atmosphere, winds sweep around the equator at 1,120 mph (1,800 km/h).

EARTH

SATURN

AXIAL TILT 26.7°

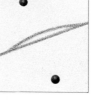

MANY MOONS

Saturn has 18 moons; one (Titan) is very large, seven are of average size, and the rest are small and irregularly shaped. Some of the small moons are co-orbital: they share an orbit with another moon. Mimas, the closest of the larger moons, is dominated by the huge crater Herschel, perhaps the result of a co-orbital collision

BRAIDED RINGS

Some of the inner moons orbit within the rings, creating gaps and braids. Pan sweeps the Enke Division clear of ring material, while Prometheus and Pandora twist and braid the F ring with their gravitational effect. These moons are sometimes said to "shepherd" the rings in the same way that dogs keep a flock of sheep together.

CROWDED SPACE

Saturn has both a pair and a triplet of co-orbital moons. In addition, two other moons, Janus and Epithemus, have orbits that are extremely close to each other. Astronomers believe that these two were once a single moon that broke up.

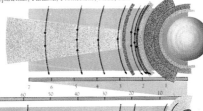

Inner moons (left to right): Helene and Dione (co-orbital); Calypso, Telesto, and Tethys (co-orbital); Enceladus; Mimas; Janus; Epithemus; Pandora; Prometheus; Atlas; Pan

Outer moons (left to right): Phoebe; Iapetus; Hyperion; Titan; Rhea; Helene; and Dione (also shown above)

SCALE IN RADIUSES OF SATURN

SATURN: SATELLITE FACTS

	Diameter		Distance from Saturn	
	miles	km	miles	km
Pan	12	20	83,033	133,600
Atlas	21	34	85,544	137,640
Prometheus	68	110	86,607	139,350
Pandora	55	88	88,067	141,700
Epimetheus	75	120	94,109	151,422
Janus	118	190	94,140	151,472
Mimas	242	390	115,301	185,520
Enceladus	311	500	147,930	238,020
Tethys	653	1,050	183,132	294,660
Telesto	15	25	183,132	294,660
Calypso	16	26	183,132	294,660
Dione	696	1,120	234,555	377,400
Helene	20	33	234,555	377,400
Rhea	951	1,530	327,557	527,040
Titan	3,201	5,150	759,385	1,221,850
Hyperion	174	280	920,447	1,481,000
Iapetus	895	1,440	2,213,362	3,561,300
Phoebe	137	220	8,049,720	12,952,000

MORE FACTS

• The rings of Saturn seem to be neatly graded, with the largest fragments found in the inner rings closest to the planet, while fine dust accumulates in the outer rings.

• Saturn is the only planet that has three moons sharing the same orbit – Tethys, Telesto, and Calypso.

• Mimas was to have been named "Arthur." Although this did not happen, many of its features are named after characters in the legend of King Arthur.

URANUS

A COLD GAS giant, Uranus is
the seventh planet from the
Sun. Little surface detail can
be seen, and even close-up
pictures show only a few
clouds of frozen methane
gas. Despite its featureless
appearance, Uranus has one
interesting peculiarity. The
planet, and its rings and
moons, are all tilted by more
than 90°, traveling around
the Sun on their side.

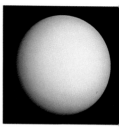

BLANK FACE
Faintly visible from Earth as a d
"star" in the night sky, Uranus
was not identified as a planet
until 1781. The ring system was
not discovered until 1977 –
almost 200 years later.

Earth

Uranus

URANUS: PLANETARY DATA

Average distance from the Sun	1,784 million miles (2,871 million km)
Orbital period	84 Earth years
Orbital velocity	4.2 miles/sec (6.8 km/s)
Rotation period	17.9 hours
Diameter at equator	31,770 miles (51,118 km)
Cloud-top temperature	–346°F (–210°C)
Mass (Earth = 1)	14.5
Gravity (Earth = 1)	0.79
Number of moons	15

URANUS FACTS

• Uranus is named after
Urania, the Greek muse
(patron goddess) of
astronomy.

• Light from the Sun,
which takes about eight
minutes to reach Earth,
takes more than 2 hours
30 minutes to travel as
far as Uranus.

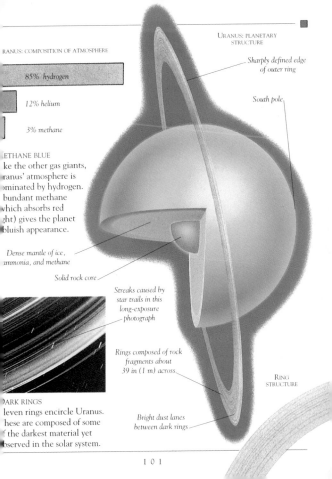

URANUS: COMPOSITION OF ATMOSPHERE

85% hydrogen

12% helium

3% methane

METHANE BLUE

Like the other gas giants,
Uranus' atmosphere is
dominated by hydrogen.
Abundant methane
(which absorbs red
light) gives the planet
its bluish appearance.

*Dense mantle of ice,
ammonia, and methane*

Solid rock core

Sharply defined edge
of outer ring

South pole

*Streaks caused by
star trails in this
long-exposure
photograph*

*Rings composed of rock
fragments about
39 in (1 m) across*

RING
STRUCTURE

DARK RINGS

Eleven rings encircle Uranus.
These are composed of some
of the darkest material yet
observed in the solar system.

*Bright dust lanes
between dark rings*

SIDEWAYS ORBIT

Uranus' axis of rotation is tilted at 98° to the vertical – the equator runs through the "top" and "bottom" of the planet. This extreme tilt also extends to the rings and moons. Uranus' sideways stance may have been the result of a collision with another celestial body at some time in the distant past.

EARTH

AXIAL TILT 98°

URANUS

LENGTHY SEASONS

Uranus' peculiar tilt create extremely long seasons. A the planet travels aroun the Sun, each pole receives 42 Earth years sunlight, followed by th same period of total darkness. However, the temperature does not vary with the seasons because Uranus is so far away from the Sun.

STRANGE MAGNETISM

Uranus generates a magnetic field which is tilted, but not the same way as the planet. The magnetic field is tilted at 60° to the axis of rotation, which means that the magnetosphere has a fairly normal shape. To make the situation even more extraordinary, Uranus' magnetic field is offset from the planet's center.

RINGS AND MOONS
Only the innermost
moon, Cordelia,
orbits within the ring
system. Miranda is
perhaps the most
unusual moon in the
solar system – it
shows every sign of
once having been
blasted apart and
then reassembled.

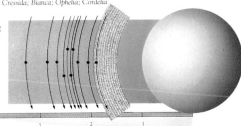

Inner moons (left to right): Puck; Belinda; Rosalind; Portia; Juliet; Desdemona; Cressida; Bianca; Ophelia; Cordelia

Outer moons (left to right): Oberon; Titania; Umbriel; Ariel; Miranda; Puck (also shown above)

URANUS: SATELLITE DATA

	Diameter		Distance from Uranus	
	miles	km	miles	km
Cordelia	19	30	30,920	49,750
Ophelia	19	30	33,412	53,760
Bianca	25	40	36,768	59,160
Cressida	43	70	38,390	61,770
Desdemona	37	60	38,943	62,660
Juliet	50	80	40,000	64,360
Portia	68	110	41,081	66,100
Rosalind	37	60	43,462	69,930
Belinda	43	70	46,774	75,260
Puck	93	150	53,456	86,010
Miranda	292	470	80,659	129,780
Ariel	721	1,160	118,856	191,240
Umbriel	727	1,170	165,301	265,970
Titania	982	1,580	270,876	435,840
Oberon	945	1,520	362,088	582,600

MORE FACTS

• Before Voyager 2,
Uranus was believed to
have five moons. The
accepted total is now
15, and there may be
more waiting to be
discovered.

• The Uranian moons
are all named after
characters in plays by
William Shakespeare.

• In contrast to Saturn,
the outermost Uranian
ring has no fragments
less than about 8 in
(20 cm) across.

NEPTUNE

THE OUTERMOST of the gas giants, Neptune is a near twin to Uranus. Too faint to be seen easily from Earth, its position was calculated mathematically. Neptune was first observed in 1846 exactly where it was predicted to be. Methane in the atmosphere gives Neptune a deep blue coloration. The rings and six of the moons were discovered by the Voyager 2 probe.

DARK STORMS
Photographed by the second Voyager probe, the atmosphere of Neptune shows several clear features including the Great Dark Spot, which is a huge cyclonic storm.

Earth

Neptune

NEPTUNE: PLANETARY DATA	
Average distance from the Sun	2,795 million miles (4,497 million km)
Orbital period	164.8 Earth years
Orbital velocity	3.4 miles/sec (5.4 km/s)
Rotation period	19.2 hours
Diameter at equator	30,782 miles (49,528 km)
Cloud-top temperature	−364°F (−220°C)
Mass (Earth = 1)	17
Gravity (Earth = 1)	1.2
Number of moons	8

NEPTUNE FACTS
• Neptune is named after the Roman god of the sea.
• Neptune radiates 2.6 times more heat than it receives from the Sun – a sign of an internal source of heat.

NEPTUNE: COMPOSITION OF ATMOSPHERE

85% hydrogen

13% helium

2% methane

HYDROCARBON HAZE
Otherwise very similar to that of Uranus,
Neptune's atmosphere has a deeper blue
color. The highest level contains a
thin hydrocarbon haze.

CIRRUS CLOUDS
High-altitude cirrus clouds of frozen
methane crystals. These clouds
are situated about
25 miles (40 km)
above the main
cloud layer.

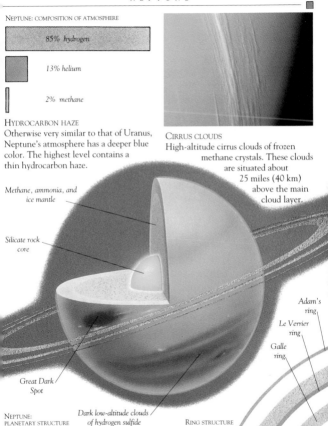

Methane, ammonia, and
ice mantle

Silicate rock
core

Adam's
ring

Le Verrier
ring

Galle
ring

Great Dark
Spot

Dark low-altitude clouds
of hydrogen sulfide

NEPTUNE:
PLANETARY STRUCTURE

RING STRUCTURE

LACK OF SEASONS
Neptune rotates on its axis at approximately the same angle of tilt as Earth. However, Neptune is far too distant from the Sun for the tilt to result in a similar cycle of seasons. Conditions in the atmosphere are dominated by winds blowing at up to 1,250 mph (2,000 km/s) which carry the dark storms around the planet in a backward direction.

EARTH

NEPTUNE

AXIAL TILT
29.6°

GREAT DARK SPOT
The largest storm on Neptune, the Great Dark Spot is about the same size as Earth. The storm rotates in an counterclockwise direction. This photograph has been processed to give a red color to high-altitude features.

TRITON
The largest of Neptune's moons, Triton is the coldest place in the solar system at −391°F (−235°C). It has a thin atmosphere, mainly of nitrogen, and a large south polar ice cap composed of methane ice. Photographs show the ice to have a pink tinge, which is believed to be due to the presence of organic chemicals formed by the action of sunlight.

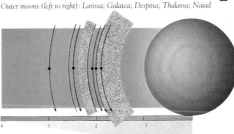

Outer moons (left to right): Larissa; Galatea; Despina; Thalassa; Naiad

CIRCLING NEPTUNE
The four innermost
moons orbit within
the ring system.
Triton is the only
large moon in the
solar system that
orbits in a backward
direction compared to
the planet's rotation.

SCALE IN RADIUSES OF NEPTUNE

Outer moons (left to right): Nereid; Triton; Proteus; Larissa; and inner moons (also shown above)

DISTANT EXPLORER
Voyager 2 is the only probe that has so far visited
Uranus and Neptune. The journey to Neptune took 12
years, and information from Voyager 2 (transmitted at
the speed of light) took more than four hours to reach
Earth. Among Voyager 2's many discoveries were six of
Neptune's eight moons and ice volcanoes on Triton.

VOYAGER 2

NEPTUNE: SATELLITE DATA				
	Diameter		Distance from Neptune	
	miles	km	miles	km
Naiad	31	50	29,832	48,000
Thalassa	50	80	31,075	50,000
Despina	112	180	32,629	52,500
Galatea	93	150	38,533	62,000
Larissa	118	190	45,743	73,600
Proteus	249	400	73,088	117,600
Triton	1,678	2,700	220,510	354,800
Nereid	211	340	3,426,600	5,513,400

FACT
• The outermost moon,
Nereid, has the most
eccentric orbit of any
known satellite. During
a single orbit, Nereid's
distance from Neptune
varies between 800,000
miles (1,300,000 km) and
6,000,000 miles
(9,700,000 km).

PLUTO

THE MOST DISTANT of all the planets, Pluto, is also the least understood. Pluto's orbit around the Sun is uniquely tilted at 17°, and is highly unusual in other ways. For about ten percent of its long orbital path, Pluto is closer to the Sun than Neptune. Pluto has a single large moon, Charon, and together they form a two-object system.

BLURRED IMAGE
The clearest image of Pluto and Charon has been obtained by the Hubble Space Telescope orbiting Earth. Ground-based photographs show a single blur.

Earth   Pluto

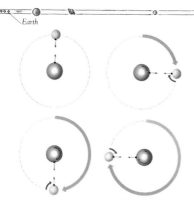

CLOSELY LINKED SYSTEM
Pluto and Charon exhibit a powerful effect on each other. Charon's orbit around Pluto has become synchronized with Pluto's own rotation, so that both have the same period – 6.4 Earth days. As a result, the same face of Charon is always turned to the same face of Pluto. From one side of Pluto, Charon is always visible in the sky. From the other side of the planet, the moon cannot be seen at all.

PLUTO: PLANETARY DATA	
Average distance from the Sun	3.675 billion miles (5.955 billion km)
Orbital period	248.5 Earth years
Orbital velocity	2.9 miles/sec (4.7 kms)
Rotation period	6.38 Earth days
Diameter at equator	1,429 miles (2,300 km)
Surface temperature	–382°F (–230°C)
Mass (Earth = 1)	0.002
Gravity (Earth = 1)	0.04 Moons: 1

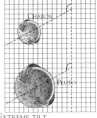

EXTREME TILT
Pluto and Charon both rotate on axes that are tilted at 122.6° to the vertical – the least upright of all the planets.

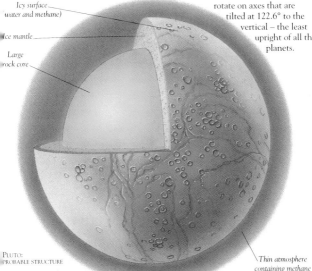

Icy surface (water and methane)

Ice mantle

Large rock core

PLUTO:
PROBABLE STRUCTURE

Thin atmosphere containing methane and nitrogen

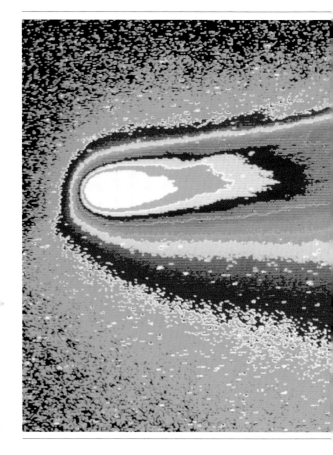

SMALL OBJECTS

COMETS

A COMET IS a "dirty snowball" composed of snow and dust. Billions of comets orbit the Sun at a distance of about one light year. A few comets have orbits that take them closer to the Sun. As they near the Sun and are heated, the snow turns to gas and forms a long bright tail.

HALLEY'S COMET
Most comets that approach the Sun are seen only once, but a few return periodically Halley's Comet returns every 76 years.

ORBITING THE SUN
A periodic comet has a regular orbit that brings it close to the Sun. For most of its orbit, the comet has no tail. The tail develops only as the comet nears the Sun and its surface is heated. The tail gets longer and longer, and then disappears as the comet moves away from the Sun.

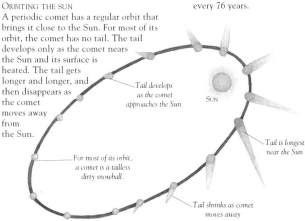

Tail develops as the comet approaches the Sun

SUN

Tail is longest near the Sun

For most of its orbit, a comet is a tailless dirty snowball.

Tail shrinks as comet moves away

GLOWING GAS

The nucleus of a typical comet is about 12.5 miles (20 km) across. When heated by the Sun, jets of gas and dust erupt from the surface of the nucleus to form a glowing cloud called a coma, which surrounds the nucleus. The coma can be ten times larger than the Earth. The comet's tail may be millions of miles (kilometers) long.

Comets often have two distinct tails, one of gas and one of dust.

Coma

Nucleus made of dust and frozen gases

Dust reflects sunlight

HEART OF A COMET

This photograph of the nucleus of Halley's Comet was taken by the Giotto probe from a distance of about 1,050 miles (1,700 km). Bright gas jets can be seen on the sunlit (upper) surface. Instruments aboard Giotto showed that the main constituent of the nucleus was ice.

COMET FACT

• The planet Jupiter is so massive that its gravity can affect the orbit of comets. In 1993, Comet Shoemaker-Levy passed close to Jupiter and was broken into several fragments by gravitational forces. During July 1994, these fragments crashed into Jupiter, causing a series of huge explosions in Jupiter's atmosphere.

METEORS

EVERY DAY, thousands of dust particles and rock fragments from space enter the Earth's atmosphere. Most burn up due to friction with the air. The streaks of light they produce are called meteors. Very rarely a larger fragment survives the atmosphere and hits Earth's surface. These "space-rocks" are called meteorites.

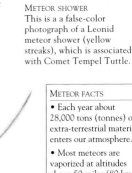

METEOR SHOWER
This is a a false-color photograph of a Leonid meteor shower (yellow streaks), which is associated with Comet Tempel Tuttle.

Earth's orbit

SUN

Elliptical comet orbit

Dust particles released by comet

CROSSING ORBITS
Most meteors are caused by dust and debris shed by comets as they pass close to the Sun. The debris stays in the path of the comet's orbit; and when the Earth's orbit crosses that of the comet, we experience a meteor shower. Some showers are regular annual events.

METEOR FACTS

• Each year about 28,000 tons (tonnes) of extra-terrestrial material enters our atmosphere.

• Most meteors are vaporized at altitudes above 50 miles (80 km).

• Meteor showers are named after the constellation in which the radiant appears, e.g. the Perseids.

• The heaviest showers, have meteors falling at 60,000 per hour.

STONY METEORITE

Fragments of nickel-iron embedded in a matrix of rock

Heat-blackened surface

STONY-IRON METEORITE

STONES AND IRONS FROM SPACE

There are two main types of meteorite – those composed mainly of rock (called "stones") and those made mostly of metal (called "irons"). Rocky meteorites are far more common than "irons," but the rarest meteorites on Earth (less than one in every hundred found) are "stony-irons" that contain both metal and rock.

IMPACT CRATER

Meteorite Crater in Arizona measures 0.8 miles (1.3 km) across. It was formed about 25,000 years ago when a meteorite about 150 ft (45 m) in diameter struck the surface at a speed of around 6.8 miles/sec (11 km/s). Meteorite hunters have found several "iron" fragments in the crater.

METEORITE FACTS

• More than 90% of identified meteorites that strike the Earth are "stones."

• The world's largest known meteorite still lies where it fell at Hoba West in southern Africa. Its weight is estimated at over 60 tons (tonnes).

• Last century, Czar Alexander of Russia had a sword made from an "iron" meteorite.

ASTEROIDS

MILLIONS OF CHUNKS of rock
orbit the Sun. These are the
asteroids, sometimes called
the minor planets. Asteroids
range in size from a few feet
(meters) across, to those that
are hundreds of miles
(kilometers) in diameter.
Most of the asteroids are
found in a wide belt between
the orbits of Mars and Jupiter.

SPACE ROCK
Ida is a typical asteroid – small
and irregular in shape with a
maximum length of 32 miles
(52 km). Its surface is heavily
cratered and covered by a thin
layer of dust.

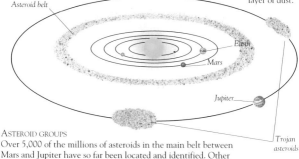

Asteroid belt

Earth

Mars

Jupiter

Trojan
asteroids

ASTEROID GROUPS
Over 5,000 of the millions of asteroids in the main belt between
Mars and Jupiter have so far been located and identified. Other
groups of asteroids follow different orbits. Trojan asteroids are
co-orbital with Jupiter, held in place by the giant planet's
powerful gravity.

Craters due to meteorite impacts

Most asteroids are irregular in shape.

...ed coloration ...cause surface is ...vered in rust

ASTEROID ORIGINS

The larger asteroids are spherical and were formed in the same way as the planets. The smaller irregular asteroids are either remnants of the original material that formed the solar system, or the result of collisions between two or more large asteroids.

FAILED PLANET

The asteroid belt was probably formed at the same time as the rest of the solar system. Rock fragments and dust particles in this part of the system were prevented from clumping together to form a planet by Jupiter's gravity. But if all the asteroids were put together, their mass would be only a tiny fraction of the Earth's.

ASTEROID FACTS

• The first asteroid to be discovered was Ceres which has a diameter of 580 miles (933 km).

• Asteroids which have an average distance from the Sun less than Earth's are known as Aten asteroids.

• Earth has been struck by several asteroids in the past, and it is only a matter of time before another asteroid strikes our planet.

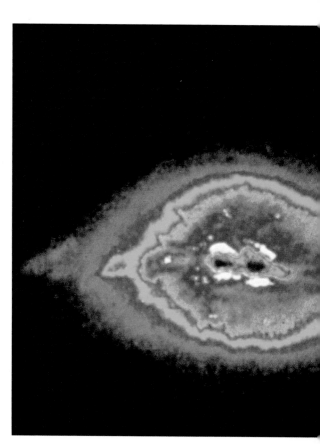

STUDYING SPACE

INFORMATION FROM SPACE

GATHERING AND STUDYING starlight is just
one way that we learn about the universe.
Visible light is only a small part of the
electromagnetic spectrum, which
covers all forms of radiation. By
studying different types of radiation,
we learn more about both the
visible and the invisible parts
of the universe.

Ozone
layer

Gamma
rays
and
X-rays

UV rays

Most infrared
stopped here

Visible light and short-
wave radio reach surface

ATMOSPHERIC SHIELD
The atmosphere shields Earth against
radiation from space. Gamma rays,
X-rays, and most ultraviolet (UV)
rays are stopped. Only visible
light, some infrared and UV
radiation, and some radio
signals reach the surface.

INFORMATION SPECTRUM
Electromagnetic radiation travels
through space as waves of
varying length (the distance
between wave crests). Gamma
rays have the shortest wavelength,
then X-rays, and so on through
the spectrum to the longest radio
waves. Visible light, which is all
that we can see naturally, occupies
a very narrow portion (less than
0.00001 percent) of the spectrum.

10^{-11} m
0.0000000000001 meters

X-RAYS

GAMMA RAYS

CRAB NEBULA IN DIFFERENT LIGHTS

The Crab Nebula is the remnant of a supernova explosion seen in 1054. In UV light (right) the nebula has an eerie glow produced by highly energetic particles from the explosion interacting with the surrounding space environment.

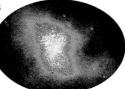

VISIBLE LIGHT

This visible light image of the nebula has been computer-processed to show the presence of hydrogen (red) and sulfur (blue) in the filaments of gas still streaming out from the explosion.

X-RAY

X-rays emitted by the Crab Nebula produce a picture (right) that shows a bright object at the center of the nebula – the pulsar that is the remains of the presupernova star.

10^{-7} m
0.0000001 meters

10^5 m
100,000 meters

VISIBLE
LIGHT

MICROWAVES

TRAVIOLET
LIGHT

INFRARED
LIGHT

RADIO
WAVES

OPTICAL TELESCOPES

THE OPTICAL TELESCOPE is one of the main tools of astronomy. But little time is spent looking through a telescope eyepiece – modern instruments collect and store visual information electronically. The optical telescope remains an important tool because it gathers basic information.

PALOMAR DOME
The protective dome of the Hale Telescope at the Mount Palomar Observatory, California, shields the telescope from the effects of weather.

Secondary mirror

Eyepiece

Main light-gathering mirror

Main light-gathering lens

Eyepiece lens

REFLECTOR TELESCOPES
Telescopes use lenses and mirrors to gather light and produce an image. Reflector telescopes, which make use of curved mirrors, are the most useful type for astronomy.

REFRACTOR TELESCOPES
Refractor telescopes use only lenses. They do not have as good light-gathering ability as reflector telescopes, but they remain very popular with amateur astronomers.

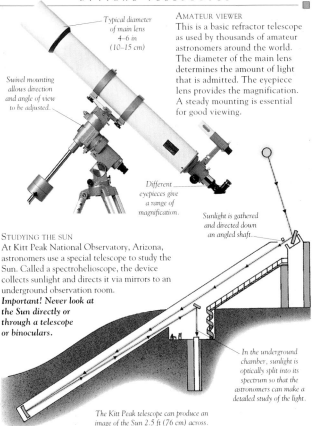

Typical diameter
of main lens
4–6 in
(10–15 cm)

Swivel mounting
allows direction
and angle of view
to be adjusted.

AMATEUR VIEWER

This is a basic refractor telescope
as used by thousands of amateur
astronomers around the world.
The diameter of the main lens
determines the amount of light
that is admitted. The eyepiece
lens provides the magnification.
A steady mounting is essential
for good viewing.

Different
eyepieces give
a range of
magnification.

Sunlight is gathered
and directed down
an angled shaft.

STUDYING THE SUN

At Kitt Peak National Observatory, Arizona,
astronomers use a special telescope to study the
Sun. Called a spectrohelioscope, the device
collects sunlight and directs it via mirrors to an
underground observation room.
**Important! Never look at
the Sun directly or
through a telescope
or binoculars.**

In the underground
chamber, sunlight is
optically split into its
spectrum so that the
astronomers can make a
detailed study of the light.

The Kitt Peak telescope can produce an
image of the Sun 2.5 ft (76 cm) across.

RADIO ASTRONOMY

WE HAVE BEEN LISTENING in to the radio energy of the universe for about 50 years. Radio astronomy can obtain additional information about familiar objects, as well as seek out new ones. Two major discoveries – quasars and pulsars – were made by radio astronomers.

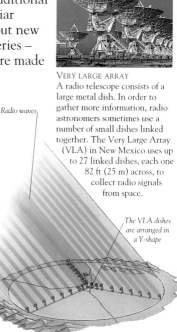

VERY LARGE ARRAY
A radio telescope consists of a large metal dish. In order to gather more information, radio astronomers sometimes use a number of small dishes linked together. The Very Large Array (VLA) in New Mexico uses up to 27 linked dishes, each one 82 ft (25 m) across, to collect radio signals from space.

Radio waves

The VLA dishes are arranged in a Y-shape

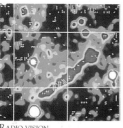

RADIO VISION
Radio telescopes, like ordinary radio sets, can be tuned to a particular wavelength, and the intensity of the radio energy can be measured. Computers are then used to produce "radio-maps" of the sky, such as this image of the bar-shaped radio source known as 1952+28.

LARGEST DISH

The world's largest radio telescope, the 1,000 ft (305 m) Arecibo dish, is built into a natural hollow in the hills of Puerto Rico. The dish is "steered" using the Earth's own rotation. Arecibo has also been used to send a radio message out into space.

Simple processing of the Arecibo message produces this visual image which contains a representation of a human being.

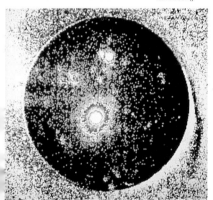

RADIO GALAXIES

Many galaxies that are quite faint visually are very "bright" at radio wavelengths. These are often called radio galaxies, or active galaxies. This optical image of radio galaxy 3C 33 has been color-coded according to the intensity of light in the visible part of the spectrum – ranging from white (most intense) to blue (the least).

IMAGES OF SPACE

MUCH OF THE information that astronomers obtain through their instruments is presented as visual images. Conventional and electronic cameras are used to record these images. The information is usually stored on computers which can process images to improve the picture and bring out details.

PIXELATED VIEW
Electronic cameras make images with a grid of tiny picture-elements (pixels). This view of a dim and distant star cluster was obtained with a ground-based telescope. The individual pixels are clearly visible, although it takes a trained eye to identify the image as a star cluster.

MARTIAN CHEMICAL PHOTOMAP
This image of the surface of Mars, with the Martian equator running across the middle of the picture, was produced by cameras aboard the Viking orbiter space probes. The image has been color-coded by computer according to the chemical composition of the surface. Craters and other surface features are also visible.

Frost is shown in turquoise

Red identifies high concentrations of iron oxide

FALSE COLOR GIVES A TRUER VIEW
Astronomers have several techniques for
analysing the information contained in
images. One of the most important is
adding false color to the image.
Saturn has a fairly muted appearance
in ordinary photographs. This
image has been color-coded to
emphasize the banding of
the planet's upper
atmosphere.

COLORING THE CORONA
This image of the normally
invisible solar corona (the Sun's
outer atmosphere) was produced
from data obtained by the Solar
Maximum Mission satellite. The
image has been computer-
processed and enhanced with
false colors, in order to identify
zones of differing gas density
within the solar corona.

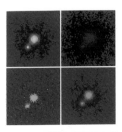

SEPARATE THEN COMBINE
Images of space are often obtained through a series
of colored filters. The object is photographed
through each filter in turn, and the resulting
images are then combined to give a much fuller
picture than with any single ordinary photograph.
This series was taken with the Hubble Space
Telescope, and shows Pluto and its moon Charon.

OBSERVATORIES

OPTICAL TELESCOPES are usually installed in mountain-top observatories, where they suffer the least interference from Earth's atmosphere. Radio telescopes can be situated almost anywhere, and are usually located near universities. Observatories are often shared between countries because of the high cost of telescopes which use the latest technology.

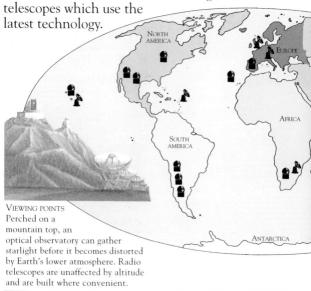

VIEWING POINTS
Perched on a mountain top, an optical observatory can gather starlight before it becomes distorted by Earth's lower atmosphere. Radio telescopes are unaffected by altitude and are built where convenient.

HIGH AND DRY
The domes of the Cerro Tololo Inter-American Observatory are sited in the Andes foothills of Chile. A dry climate with cloud-free nights and a steady atmosphere makes this an ideal location for clear viewing.

ASIA

AUSTRALASIA

MAP KEY

OPTICAL TELESCOPE

RADIO TELESCOPE

OBSERVATORY FACTS

• The oldest existing observatory was built in South Korea in AD 632.

• There is a flying telescope – the Kuiper Airborne Observatory, a modified C-141 cargo aircraft fitted with a 36 in (91 cm) telescope.

• The 36 elements of the Keck reflector make a mirror 396 in (1,000 cm) across.

• The world's highest observatory is located near Boulder, Colorado, 14,110 ft (4,297 m) above sea level.

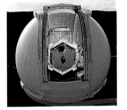

HIGH-TECH TELESCOPE
The Keck Telescope situated on Mauna Kea, Hawaii, is the world's largest optical telescope. The main mirror is made up of 36 computer-controlled hexagonal segments.

TELESCOPES IN SPACE

BY PLACING THEIR TELESCOPES in orbit above Earth's atmosphere, astronomers get a much better view. They can see farther and can collect information from wavelengths that are absorbed by the atmosphere. Information and images gathered in orbit are transmitted back to Earth for study and analysis.

ORBITING TELESCOPE
The US space station Skylab carried a total of eight telescopes on the X-shaped Apollo Telescope Mounting

Large solar panels power the equipment aboard the HST.

Antenna transmits information to Earth via a communications satellite

Protective hinged cover

NASA

esa

Cameras and instruments located inside

HUBBLE
The Hubble Space Telescope (HST) uses a large mirror to gather light. The light is then directed by a secondary mirror into one of the scientific instrument packages or high-resolution cameras aboard this orbiting space telescope

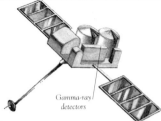

Gamma-ray
detectors

DIRECTION FINDER

Orbiting gamma-ray telescopes
(left) have been in use since the
mid-1970s. Although gamma rays
cannot be focused to produce an
image, they can be used to plot
the direction and intensity of
gamma-ray sources.

SPECIAL TELESCOPES

Orbiting X-ray satellites (right) enable
scientists to pinpoint areas of intense activity
in distant galaxies. Special telescopes, known
as grazing incidence telescopes, are used
because X-rays pass straight through
conventional lenses and mirrors.

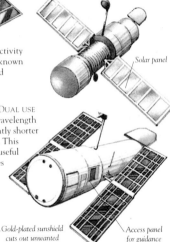

Solar panel

DUAL USE

The HST (right) operates at the wavelength
of visible light, and also at the slightly shorter
ultraviolet (UV) wavelength. This
feature makes the HST doubly useful
to astronomers as data and images
obtained at two different
wavelengths can be compared.

Access panel
for guidance
package

Gold-plated sunshield
cuts out unwanted
infrared radiation

CLEARER VIEW

From orbit, infrared telescopes (left)
gather infrared light before it can be
absorbed by Earth's lower atmosphere.
Infrared satellites are also used to study
the Earth's surface.

ROCKETS

SATELLITES, SPACE PROBES, and astronauts are lifted into space by rockets. There are two main types. The conventional tall, thin rocket is made from several stages stacked on top of each other. The newer Space Shuttle design lifts off with the aid of massive booster rockets. But when it returns from space, the Shuttle lands like an aircraft.

LIFTOFF
A Saturn V rocket stands poised on the launch-pad. Its engines burn fuel at a rate of thousands of gallons (liters) per second.

Nozzle shapes the stream of hot exhaust gases.

Liquid fuel and oxygen are combined in the combustion chamber.

Fuel tank

Oxygen tank

Fuel and oxygen stored in reinforced pressurised tanks

Pumps control the flow of fuel and oxygen to the combustion chamber.

ROCKET POWER
A rocket is propelled upward by hot exhaust gases streaming from nozzles at the tail. These gases are the result of burning a mixture of liquid oxygen and fuel (such as liquid hydrogen) inside a combustion chamber. Carrying its own oxygen supply enables a rocket engine to function in the airless vacuum of space.

ESCAPE VELOCITY

A rocket, or any other object, is held on the Earth's surface by the force of gravity. To escape the effects of Earth's gravity and enter space, a rocket needs to achieve a speed of 24,840 mph (40,000 km/h) – this is the "escape velocity" of planet Earth. On the Moon, where the force of gravity is only one sixth as powerful as on Earth, the escape velocity is lower – only about 5,300 mph (8,500 km/h).

Payload – satellite or space probe

Third-stage rocket engines

ARIANE: A TYPICAL THREE-STAGE LAUNCH VEHICLE

Second-stage rocket engines

First-stage rocket engines

External booster rockets assist first stage engines at liftoff

REUSABLE SPACE CRAFT

A streaming exhaust trail marks the beginning of another Space Shuttle mission. Unlike conventional rockets, which can be used only once, the Shuttle is reusable. The massive fuel tank and booster rockets are jettisoned shortly after launch and recovered. The Shuttle's own engines carry it on into orbit, and small thruster rockets are used to maneuver it into position.

FLY-BYS

LIFTED INTO SPACE by rockets, space probes are computer-controlled robots packed with scientific instruments. Probes are sent to fly by a planet, or even orbit around it, sending data and images back to Earth. After they have completed their planned missions, some probes continue on into space.

VOLCANIC DISCOVERY
The probe Voyager I obtained this image of Io which shows the first active volcano seen outside Earth.

Three probes used Saturn's gravity to accelerate their journey.

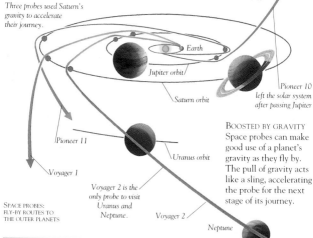

Earth

Jupiter orbit

Saturn orbit

Pioneer 10
left the solar system after passing Jupiter

Pioneer 11

Voyager 1

Uranus orbit

Voyager 2 is the only probe to visit Uranus and Neptune.

Voyager 2

Neptune

BOOSTED BY GRAVITY
Space probes can make good use of a planet's gravity as they fly by. The pull of gravity acts like a sling, accelerating the probe for the next stage of its journey.

SPACE PROBES:
FLY-BY ROUTES TO
THE OUTER PLANETS

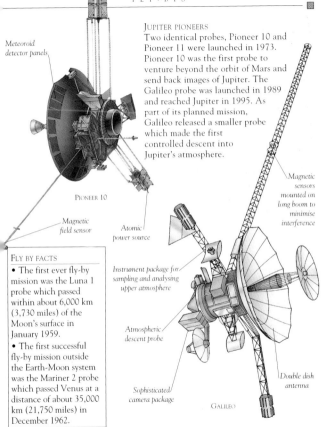

JUPITER PIONEERS

Two identical probes, Pioneer 10 and
Pioneer 11 were launched in 1973.
Pioneer 10 was the first probe to
venture beyond the orbit of Mars and
send back images of Jupiter. The
Galileo probe was launched in 1989
and reached Jupiter in 1995. As
part of its planned mission,
Galileo released a smaller probe
which made the first
controlled descent into
Jupiter's atmosphere.

Meteoroid
detector panels

PIONEER 10

Magnetic
field sensor

Atomic
power source

Magnetic
sensors
mounted on
long boom to
minimise
interference

Instrument package for
sampling and analysing
upper atmosphere

Atmospheric
descent probe

Double dish
antenna

Sophisticated
camera package

GALILEO

FLY BY FACTS

• The first ever fly-by
mission was the Luna 1
probe which passed
within about 6,000 km
(3,730 miles) of the
Moon's surface in
January 1959.
• The first successful
fly-by mission outside
the Earth-Moon system
was the Mariner 2 probe
which passed Venus at a
distance of about 35,000
km (21,750 miles) in
December 1962.

LANDERS

SPACE PROBES SENT to orbit a
planet can release a second
craft to land on the surface.
The lander, a scientific robot,
carries out its preprogrammed
tasks and then relays the data
it has obtained back to Earth.
So far, landers have provided
information about the Moon,
Venus, and Mars.

COMING IN TO LAND
This dramatic photograph of
lunar craters was taken from
one of the Apollo landers
during its low-altitude descent
to the Moon's surface.

IS THERE LIFE ON MARS?
Two Viking orbiter craft each
released a lander that descended
safely to the Martian surface. In total
about 3,000 photographic images
were sent back to Earth. The landers
also tested the Martian soil with four
different experiments to check for
any signs of life – none
was found.

VIKING LANDER CRAFT

Television cameras

Sensors for
testing atmospheric
conditions

Robot arm to
take soil samples

The two parts separate
and the lander
begins its descent
through the atmosphere.

The protective
atmospheric shield
is jettisoned

VENERA 9 LANDER CRAFT

On-board braking
engines begin to slow
Venera 9

LANDER FACTS

• The first successful
lander was Luna 9,
which soft-landed on
the Moon in 1966.

• Venera 7 became the
first lander to transmit
data from the surface of
Venus in 1970.

• The Viking landers
analysed Mars' soil and
found that it contained
the following chemical
elements:

silica	14%
iron	18%
aluminum	2.7%
titanium	0.9%
potassium	0.3%

HOT LANDING

A series of Venera space
probes was sent to Venus.
Each consisted of two parts,
one of which descended to
the surface. Conditions on
Venus – very high temperature
and pressure – meant that
the landers could function
only for a few minutes.

Parachutes
further slow the
descent

Venera 9 obtains
and transmits
several images
before failing

WORKING IN SPACE

ASTRONAUTS NOW WORK in
space on a regular basis. Many
experiments are carried out
aboard orbiting laboratories;
and satellites are launched,
retrieved, and repaired while
in Earth orbit.

WORKING ON THE MOON
Buzz Aldrin (the second man
to walk on the Moon) sets
up one of the scientific
experiment packages that
the Apollo 11 crew left
behind on the lunar surface.

Television camera

Steering control

Antenna

Equipment storage rack

Wire-mesh wheels

LUNAR ROVING VEHICLE
(LRV)

MOON BUGGY
Crew members of the
Apollo 15, 16, and 17
missions made effective
use of the LRV. This
"moon-buggy" enabled
them to travel tens of
miles (kilometers)
across the lunar surface
collecting samples over
a wide area.

SELF-PROPELLED
Powered by small jets
of nitrogen gas, the
Manned Maneuvering
Unit enables astronauts
to move about freely
outside their spacecraft.

MANNED
MANEUVERING
UNIT

ORBITING WORKPLACE

Space stations are both home and workplace for astronauts. Mir was launched by the Soviet Union in 1986 and has been visited by several crews of astronauts who have stayed aboard for weeks or months at a time.

Solar panel

Docking port for supply craft

Living quarters with washing and toilet area

Science and astronomy area

LABORATORY CONDITIONS

A crew member places a specimen inside one of the zero-gravity experiment chambers located in the Space Shuttle's crew compartment. Larger scale experiments can be carried out in the cargo bay using computer-controlled equipment.

RUNNING REPAIRS

The Space Shuttle lets astronauts position themselves alongside a faulty satellite and either repair it in space, or bring it back to Earth for overhaul. The most successful repair mission to date was in December 1993, when new optical equipment was installed on the Hubble Space Telescope.

SPACE
HISTORY

MILESTONES IN ASTRONOMY

The astronomer's job is to observe, describe, and explain objects in space. The story of astronomy is marked by a series of milestone achievements. Advances in technology have led to better descriptions and more comprehensive explanations.

EUDOXUS OF CNIDUS (408-355 B.C.) was a Greek thinker who studied at Athens under the philosopher Plato. In later life he developed the theory of crystal spheres – the first scientific attempt to explain the observed motion of the planets, and stars.

MILESTONE
According to Eudoxus, the Earth was at the center of the universe. The stars and planets were set into a series of transparent crystal spheres that surrounded the Earth in space.

PTOLEMY (C.A.D. 120-180) lived in Alexandria, Egypt, at the height of the Roman Empire. Although little is known about him, he has become famous as the "father of astronomy." The idea that the Earth is at the center of the universe is often referred to as the "Ptolemaic System."

MILESTONE
He compiled a compendium, known as the "Almagest," of ancient Greek astronomical knowledge. Handed down over the centuries, Ptolemy's book continued to provide the basis of scientific astronomy for more than 1,000 years.

AL-SUFI (903-86) was a Persian nobleman, and one of the leading astronomers of his time. His "Book of Fixed Stars" listed the position and brightness of more than 1,000 stars, and beautifully illustrated the main constellations.

MILESTONE
During the Dark Ages, scientific astronomy was kept alive in the Islamic empire. Our knowledge of the works of Ptolemy is entirely due to Arab translators.

NICOLAUS COPERNICUS (1473-1543) worked as a church lawyer in Poland. Near the end of his life he published an exciting new view of the universe which replaced Ptolemy's.

MILESTONE
Copernicus removed the Earth from its traditional place at the center of the universe, and replaced it with the Sun. This was considered to be revolutionary view, and the "Copernican Revolution" was strongly opposed by the Christian Church.

GALILEO GALILEI (1564-1642) was an Italian scientist and astronomer who supported Copernicus' new theory. As a result, he was put on trial by the Church, and he remained a virtual prisoner for the rest of his life.

MILESTONE
Galileo pioneered the use of the refractor telescope for astronomy. He made several major discoveries, including mountains on the Moon, the phases of Venus, and the four largest moons of Jupiter.

ISAAC NEWTON (1643-1727) was a professor of mathematics and a great scientist. He is supposed to have had the idea for his theory of gravity after seeing an apple fall from a tree.

MILESTONE
The theory of gravity explained why apples fall, and why planets orbit around the Sun. Newton was able to establish the scientific laws that apply to the motion of objects in space. He also experimented with optics – splitting sunlight into its spectrum – and designed a reflecting telescope.

EDMOND HALLEY (1656-1742) became Britain's Astronomer Royal – one of the first official government scientists. As a young man he voyaged to the remote island of St. Helena, and charted the stars of the Southern Hemisphere.

MILESTONE
Halley is famous for predicting the return of the periodic comet that now bears his name. His work reinforced the idea that astronomy is a very precise science that can make accurate predictions.

WILLIAM HERSCHEL (1738-1822) was born in Hanover, Germany, but moved to England where he at first worked as a professional musician. His interest in astronomy led him to design and build his own telescopes.

MILESTONE
Herschel became famous for his discovery of the planet Uranus in 1781. Today he is remembered as one of the greatest astronomical observers. By studying the Milky Way over many years, he was able to make the first reasonably accurate estimate of its size and shape.

JOSEPH VON FRAUNHOFER (1787-1826) was an orphan who eventually became the director of a scientific institute in Germany. He was a trained optical worker who made some of the world's highest-quality telescope lenses.

MILESTONE
Fraunhofer identified and studied the dark absorption lines (now called Fraunhofer lines) in the solar spectrum. These lines enable scientists to tell which chemical elements are present in a source of light.

NEPTUNE (FIRST LOCATED IN 1846) The position of a new planet in the solar system was predicted mathematically. But its existence could not be confirmed until it had been observed.

MILESTONE
The "discovery" of Neptune was made possible by astronomers' increased understanding of the universe. Following the work of Newton and Halley, they were able to make increasingly accurate predictions about the behavior of objects in space.

WILLIAM HUGGINS (1824-1910) was an English astronomer who had his own private observatory in London. He was a pioneer of the technique of stellar spectroscopy (analysing the spectra produced by starlight).

MILESTONE
Huggins studied the light from many different stars. As a result of his work, he was able to show that stars are made of the same chemical elements that are found on Earth. He also showed that some nebulae are composed of gas.

GIOVANNI SCHIAPARELLI (1835-1910) was an Italian astronomer who became director of the Brera Observatory at Turin. He made headlines in 1877, when he claimed to be able to see a network of canals on Mars.

MILESTONE
Schiaparelli's most famous discovery was mistaken, but it did focus popular interest and attention on astronomy. He also established the link between comets and meteor showers.

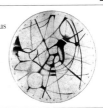

EJNAR HERTZSPRUNG (1873-1967) and HENRY RUSSELL (1877-1957) were two scientists who, working independently, came to the same conclusions about the color and temperature of stars.

MILESTONE
The Hertzsprung-Russell (HR) diagram shows the relationship between surface temperature and color. Astronomers can identify the so-called "main sequence" of stellar development. Giant, supergiant, and dwarf stars are also located on the diagram.

ARTHUR EDDINGTON (1882-1945) was born in the north of England and became Professor of Astronomy at Cambridge. He was interested in the origin of stars, and he wrote science books for a general audience.

MILESTONE
Eddington was able to describe the structure of a star. He also explained how a star stays in one piece – balanced by the forces of gravity (pulling in), and gas pressure and radiation pressure (pushing out).

HARLOW SHAPLEY (1885-1972) was an American astronomer who became director of Harvard College Observatory. He used various stars as markers to study the distance and distribution of star clusters.

MILESTONE
Shapley was able to give the first accurate estimate of the size and shape of the Milky Way galaxy. He also showed that the Sun is located a very long way from the center of the galaxy.

CECILIA PAYNE-GAPOSCHKIN (1900-79) was born in England, but spent most of her working life at Harvard Observatory in the US. She is thought by many people to have been the greatest ever woman astronomer.

MILESTONE
By analysing the spectra of many different stars, Payne-Gaposchkin was able to show that all stars in the main sequence of development (the Sun for example) are composed almost entirely of the chemical elements hydrogen and helium.

EDWIN HUBBLE (1889-1953) was an American who began his working life as a lawyer before becoming a professional astronomer. He showed that the Andromeda spiral was definitely not part of the Milky Way galaxy.

MILESTONE
By showing that some objects are located outside the Milky Way, Hubble proved the existence of other galaxies. He also discovered that the universe appears to be constantly expanding.

GEORGES LEMAITRE (1894-1966) was a Belgian mathematician who worked in Britain and the US. His work had an important influence on the way that astronomers think about the universe.

MILESTONE
Lemaître proposed and developed the Big Bang theory about the origin of the universe. According to this theory, all matter and energy were created simultaneously by a huge explosion. This theory explains why many galaxies appear to be speeding away from us.

KARL JANSKY (1905-49) was an American radio engineer. While trying to solve the problem of static and interference with radio broadcasts, he discovered radio waves coming from the Milky Way.

MILESTONE
Without realizing it, Jansky discovered the basic techniques of radio astronomy. As a result of his work, astronomers have been able to to gather information from other parts of the electromagnetic spectrum, and not just from visible light.

FRED HOYLE (b. 1915) is a British astronomer who began his career as a mathematician. He became famous for his theory that life on Earth was the result of infection by bacteria from space carried by comets.

MILESTONE
Hoyle's most important work concerned the basic nuclear reactions at work deep inside stars. He explained the processes by which stars convert hydrogen into helium and other heavier elements.

FRED WHIPPLE (b. 1906) was appointed professor of astronomy at Harvard in 1945, and became director of the Smithsonian Astrophysical Observatory in 1955. He is best known for his studies of comets and the solar system.

MILESTONE
His theory that comets are "dirty snowballs" has recently been proved correct by space probes such as Giotto. It now seems likely that comets are "leftovers" from the formation of the solar system.

ARNO PENZIAS (b. 1933) AND ROBERT WILSON (b. 1936) are American scientists. In 1978 they received the Nobel prize for physics for discovering the background radio energy of the universe – energy that is left over from the Big Bang.

MILESTONE
This radio energy ("the microwave background") gives the universe an average temperature about 5°F (3°C) above absolute zero. Many people believe that its discovery confirmed the Big Bang theory.

SUPERNOVA 1987A
The observation of a bright supernova during 1987 gave astronomers their first opportunity to study a supernova event with modern telescopes and other equipment.

MILESTONE
Analysis of the energy and particles produced by the event confirmed the theory that all chemical elements heavier than iron are made by very high-temperature nuclear reactions during supernova explosions.

SPACE MISSIONS I

THE SPACE AGE began in 1957 with the launch of the first satellite. Four years later Yuri Gagarin became the world's first astronaut. The next 20 years saw a surge of interest in space exploration.

FIRST SPACE VEHICLE
A model of Vostok 1, the craft in which Yuri Gagarin made his historic first orbit of the Earth on April 12, 1961.

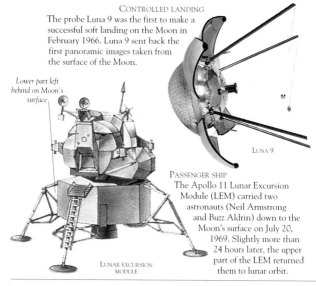

CONTROLLED LANDING
The probe Luna 9 was the first to make a successful soft landing on the Moon in February 1966. Luna 9 sent back the first panoramic images taken from the surface of the Moon.

Lower part left behind on Moon's surface

LUNA 9

PASSENGER SHIP
The Apollo 11 Lunar Excursion Module (LEM) carried two astronauts (Neil Armstrong and Buzz Aldrin) down to the Moon's surface on July 20, 1969. Slightly more than 24 hours later, the upper part of the LEM returned them to lunar orbit.

LUNAR EXCURSION MODULE

ROBOT MOON ROVER
Two Lunokhod robot vehicles
were sent to the Moon in the
early 1970s. Equipped with
television cameras that enabled
them to be driven from a control
room on Earth, the two vehicles
traveled a total of 29.5 miles
(47.5 km) across the Moon.

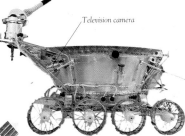

Television camera

LUNOKHOD 1

*Apollo
Telescope
Mount*

SKYLAB

SCIENTIFIC PLATFORM
Launched in 1973, the Skylab
orbiting laboratory and observatory
gave astronauts the opportunity to
work in space for weeks at a time.
Skylab also enabled scientists to
study the workings of Earth's
atmosphere and climate systems
from the viewpoint of space.

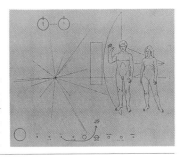

MESSAGE TO THE STARS
The two Pioneer probes each
carry a gold-covered plaque that
shows a visual representation of
human beings, as well as simple
directions for locating the solar
system and planet Earth.

SPACE MISSIONS II

WORKING IN ORBIT became much
easier with the introduction of
the Space Shuttle in 1981.
Probes have now visited all but
one of the outer planets, and
further exploration
is planned.

*The Shuttle has a
mechanical arm which
can be used to launch
or retrieve satellites.*

*The external fuel
tank breaks away
at a height of
70 miles (110 km).*

*The booster rockets operate
for about two minutes and
are jettisoned at a height
of 28 miles (45 km).*

*The Shuttle can lift
off with eight crew
and up to 29 tons
(tonnes) of cargo.*

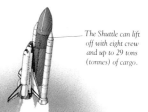

INCREASING COMMUNICATIONS

The communications satellite Intelsat
was launched by astronauts on the 49th
Space Shuttle mission in May 1992.
Improved communications is just one of
the benefits of space technology now
enjoyed by the general public.

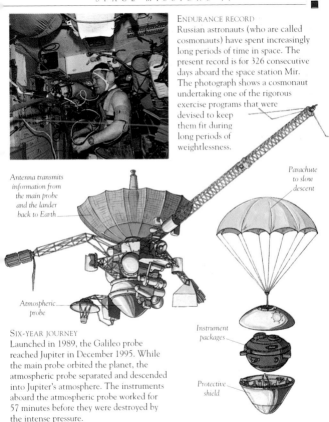

ENDURANCE RECORD
Russian astronauts (who are called cosmonauts) have spent increasingly long periods of time in space. The present record is for 326 consecutive days aboard the space station Mir. The photograph shows a cosmonaut undertaking one of the rigorous exercise programs that were devised to keep them fit during long periods of weightlessness.

Antenna transmits information from the main probe and the lander back to Earth

Parachute to slow descent

Atmospheric probe

Instrument packages

Protective shield

SIX-YEAR JOURNEY
Launched in 1989, the Galileo probe reached Jupiter in December 1995. While the main probe orbited the planet, the atmospheric probe separated and descended into Jupiter's atmosphere. The instruments aboard the atmospheric probe worked for 57 minutes before they were destroyed by the intense pressure.

Glossary

ABSORPTION LINES
Thin dark lines across a spectrum which indicate the presence of chemical elements in the light source.

ACCRETION DISK
A structure formed by material being drawn into a rapidly rotating black hole.

ASTEROID
A lump of rock orbiting the Sun. Most asteroids are found in a narrow belt situated between Mars and Jupiter.

ASTRONAUT
Someone who travels through space.

ASTRONOMY
The scientific study of objects in space.

ATMOSPHERE
Layer of gases surrounding a planet, moon, or star.

AXIS (OF SPIN)
An imaginary line through a rotating object, around which the object rotates.

BIG BANG
The explosion that created the universe about 15 billion years ago.

BIG CRUNCH
One possible future end for the universe – the Big Bang in reverse.

BLACK HOLE
An infinitely dense object formed initially by the collapse of a massive star. The gravity of a black hole is so strong that not even light can escape from it.

CELESTIAL EQUATOR
A projection of Earth's equator out into space, used as a baseline for positioning stars.

CELESTIAL POLE
Projection of Earth's north or south pole into space, for use as a reference point.

CELESTIAL SPHERE
The appearance of the stars from Earth – as though they were set into a black sphere around the planet.

CHROMOSPHERE
The Sun's inner atmosphere.

CLUSTER
A grouping of stars or galaxies held by gravity.

COMET
An object composed of snow and dust that orbits the Sun. If a comet approaches the Sun it forms a tail of gas and dust particles.

CONSTELLATION
A grouping of bright stars seen in Earth's sky. In most cases the grouping is a trick of perspective and the stars are a long way apart.

CO-ORBITAL
Sharing an orbital path with another object.

CORE
The central region of a planet, star, or galaxy.

CORONA
The Sun's outer atmosphere.

CRATER
Circular depression in the surface of a planet or a moon caused by a meteorite impact.

CRUST
The surface layer of a rock planet or moon.

ECLIPSE
The effect produced when one object in space passes in front of another and obscures it.

ECLIPTIC
The Sun's apparent path around the celestial sphere during a year.

ELECTROMAGNETIC SPECTRUM
The spectrum of radiated energy which includes: gamma rays, X-rays, ulraviolet rays, visible light, infrared radiation, microwaves, and radio and television signals.

ESCAPE VELOCITY
The velocity needed to overcome a planet's, or a moon's, gravity.

FLYBY
The path of a space probe that obtains information by flying past, or orbiting, a moon or planet.

GALAXY
A large grouping of stars held together by gravity. Galaxies can be spiral, elliptical (oval), or irregular in shape.

GRAVITY
An attractive force that is a property of mass.

GREENHOUSE EFFECT
Increased heating of a planetary atmosphere due to an excess of carbon dioxide.

HELIOSPHERE
The volume of space swept by charged particles from the Sun.

HEMISPHERE
One half of a sphere. The term is usually applied to regions north or south of an equator.

LIGHT-YEAR (LY)
The distance traveled by light in one year – used to measure distances between stars and galaxies.

LOCAL ARM
Name often given to the Orion arm – the spiral arm of the Milky Way galaxy in which the Sun is located.

LOCAL GROUP
The cluster of galaxies of which the Milky Way galaxy is a member.

LUMINOSITY
The amount of light energy produced by a light source.

MAGNETIC FIELD
The region around a magnetic source within which the magnetic force operates.

MAGNETOSPHERE
The volume of space influenced by a planet's magnetic field.

MAGNITUDE
The brightness of a star or galaxy. Apparent magnitude is the brightness as actually seen from Earth. Absolute magnitude is the brightness if seen from a standard distance of about 32.5 light years.

MAIN SEQUENCE
A stage in the life cycle of stars during which they produce energy through the conversion of hydrogen to helium.

MANTLE
The molten middle layer of a rock planet.

MASS
The amount of matter in an object. The Sun's mass (1 solar mass) is used as a standard for measuring the mass of stars and galaxies.

MATTER
Anything that occupies space. There are three states of matter– gas, liquid, and solid.

MESSIER CATALOGUE
A list of bright clusters, galaxies, and nebulae compiled in 1781.

METEOR
A streak of light in the sky caused by a rock or dust particle from space burning up because of atmospheric friction.

METEORITE
A piece of rock or metal from space that impacts on the surface of a planet or moon.

METEOROID
A fragment of rock or metal in space.

MILKY WAY
The spiral galaxy which contains billions of stars including the Sun.

MINOR PLANETS
Old name for asteroids.

MOON
A natural satellite of a planet. Earth's moon is the Moon.

NEBULA
A cloud of gas and dust in space. Some nebulae glow, others are dark.

NEUTRON STAR
A star that has collapsed into a super-dense form of matter. Some neutron stars are seen as pulsars.

NEW GENERAL CATALOGUE
A list of clusters, galaxies, and nebulae first published in 1888.

NUCLEAR FUSION
The power source of stars. A reaction in which atoms fuse together giving off large amounts of energy.

NUCLEUS
The central part of an atom, comet, or galaxy.

OBSERVATORY
A building that contains an astronomical telescope.

ORBIT
The path of one object in space around another.

ORBITAL PERIOD
The time taken for an object to make one complete orbit.

ORBITAL VELOCITY
The velocity required to maintain an orbit.

PARALLAX METHOD
A way of calculating the distance to stars by measuring the apparent shift in their position.

PENUMBRA
The outer part of the shadow cast during an eclipse of the Sun. Also,

the outer and warmer part of a sunspot.

PERIODIC COMET
A comet that comes close to the Sun at regular intervals.

PHOTOSPHERE
The Sun's visible surface.

PLANET
A spherical object, composed of rock or liquefied gas, that orbits around a star.

PRESSURE
The force acting on a given area of surface.

PROMINENCE
A jet of gas arising from the Sun's surface.

PROTON-PROTON CHAIN
The main type of fusion reaction inside stars whereby hydrogen is converted into helium.

PROTOSTAR
A very young star that has not begun to shine.

PULSAR
A rapidly rotating neutron star that gives off beams of energy.

QUASAR
A very bright and distant object believed to be the core of a very young galaxy.

RADAR-MAPPING
A technique for producing relief maps from radar signals.

RADIANT
The point in the sky from which a meteor shower appears to come.

RADIATION
Forms of energy able to travel across space.

RED GIANT
A stage in the life cycle of many stars when they increase in size and begin the conversion of helium to carbon.

RED SHIFT
A shift towards the red end of the spectrum seen in light from sources that are moving away from the Earth.

ROTATION PERIOD
The time taken for an object to make one complete axial rotation.

SATELLITE
An object orbiting around a planet. There are natural satellites (moons), and artificial satellites put in orbit by human beings.

SOLAR PANELS
Electronic devices that produce electricity when placed in sunlight.

SOLAR SYSTEM
The Sun, and all the planets, moons, asteroids, and comets that orbit around it.

SOLAR WIND
A stream of electrically charged particles given off by the Sun.

SPACE
The volume between objects in the universe.

SPECTROHELIOSCOPE
A special telescope for studying the Sun.

SPECTRUM
Display of the different wavelengths or frequencies that make up radiated energy.

STAR
A large spinning ball of very hot gas which generates energy by nuclear fusion.

SUNSPOTS
Dark, irregular patches that are visible on the Sun's surface.

SUPERCLUSTER
A huge cluster that is itself made up of clusters of galaxies.

SUPERNOVA
The explosion of a large star which may briefly produce more light than an entire galaxy.

TELESCOPE
A device for seeing at a distance. Optical telescopes use mirrors and lenses. Radio telescopes use metal dishes to "see" radio signals. Other telescopes are sensitive to other forms of energy.

UMBRA
The inner part of the shadow cast during a solar or lunar eclipse. Also, the inner and cooler part of a sunspot.

UNIVERSE
Everything that exists.

VACUUM
Space empty of matter.

WAVELENGTH
A characteristic feature of radiant energy.

WEIGHTLESSNESS
Condition of apparent zero gravity experienced by space travelers.

WHITE DWARF
The collapsed core of a Sun-sized star.

ZODIAC
The 12 constellations through which the Sun appears to travel during one year.

Index

Acknowledgements

Dorling Kindersley would like to thank:
Caroline Potts for sympathetic photo-librarianship, Robert Graham , Ray Rogers and Connie Mersel for cheerful assistance, Hilary Bird for the index, and Dr. David W. Hughes of Sheffield University for his much appreciated professional advice.

Illustrations by:
Rick Blakely, Luciano Corbella, Richard Draper, Mike Grey, Jeremy Gower, John Hutchinson, Andrew Macdonald, J. Marffy, Daniel J. Pyne, Pete Serjeant, Guy Smith, Taurus Graphics, Raymond Turvey, François Vincent, Richard Ward, Brian Watson, John Woodcock

Picture credits: t = top b = bottom c = center l = left r = right
Anglo Australian Telescope Board/D.Malin 37tr, 42/43, Rob Beighton 83cl, The Bodleian Library, University of Oxford 142bl, ESO/Meylan 126tr, 130b, 137tl, 139t, Mary Evans Picture Library 142cl, 143tr, 143crb, 143 br, 144-145; FLPA 46tr, Genesis Space Photo Library 10/11, 127t, Harvard University Archives 146t, Image Select/Ann Ronan 142-145, JPL courtesy of NOAO 112tl, Lund Observatory 25tl, Mansell Collection 143rct, 144-145, NASA/JPL 13tr, 16bl, 20tl, 21tr, 24tr, 27tr, 28/29, 30tr, 32tr, 54tr, 60/61, 66tr, 68bl, 70/71, 72tr, 73tl, 76tr, 77tr, 79tl, 80tl, 81tl, 84tl, 85tl, 88tr, 89tr, 90cl, 92tr, 93tr, 96tr, 97tr, 98cl, 100tr, 101bl, 104tr, 105tr, 106cl, 108tr, 118/119, 121tr, 121cr, 126b, 127c, 127b, 130tr, 132tr, 133cl, 134tr, 136tr, 138tr, 138br, 139cr, 139bl, 140/141, 144clb, 147cb, 148/149, 149cl, 150cr, Novosti 151tl, Science Photo Library/ Alex Bariel 122tr, Dr. Jeremy Burgess 142tl, ESA 113br, Fred Espenak 45t, François Gohier 124tr, Max Planck Institut fur Radioastronomy 124bl, 146b, David Mclean 114tr, NASA 116tr, NOAO 18/19, 121c, Pekka Parviainen 47tl, Roger Ressmeyer, Starlight 44tr, Royal Observatory Edinburgh/Anglo-Australian Telescope Board 22tr, 26bl, 50tr, 110/111; Royal Greenwich Observatory 125cl, John Sanford 48tr, 115br, Dr. Seth Shostak 125tl, Starland Picture Library/ESO 35tl, UPI/Bettman 146cr.

Every effort has been made to trace the copyright holders and we apologize in advance for any unintentional omissions. We would be pleased to insert the appropriate acknowledgement in any subsequent edition of this publication.